The Most
Beautiful House
in the World

The Most Beautiful House in the World

BY

WITOLD
RYBCZYNSKI

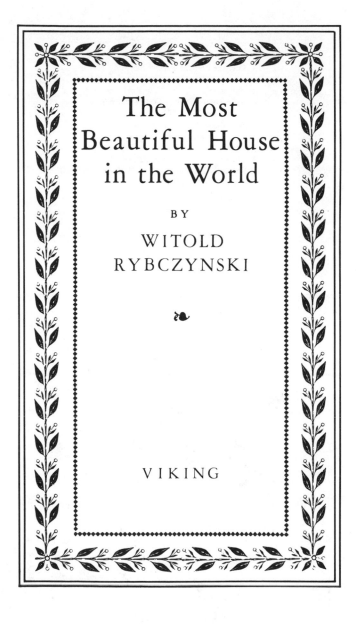

VIKING

VIKING
Published by the Penguin Group
Viking Penguin, a division of Penguin Books USA Inc.,
40 West 23rd Street, New York, New York 10010, U.S.A.
Penguin Books Ltd, 27 Wrights Lane,
London W8 5TZ, England
Penguin Books Australia Ltd, Ringwood,
Victoria, Australia
Penguin Books Canada Ltd, 2801 John Street,
Markham, Ontario, Canada L3R 1B4
Penguin Books (N.Z.) Ltd, 182–190 Wairau Road,
Auckland 10, New Zealand

Penguin Books Ltd, Registered Offices:
Harmondsworth, Middlesex, England

First published in 1989 by Viking Penguin,
a division of Penguin Books USA Inc.
Published simultaneously in Canada

3 5 7 9 10 8 6 4

Library of Congress Cataloging in Publication Data
Rybczynski, Witold.
The most beautiful house in the world.
Bibliography: p.
Includes index.
1. Architecture, Domestic.   2. Rybczynski, Witold—
Homes and haunts.   I. Title.
NA7120.R93   1989   728.3'73'0924   88-40400
ISBN 0-670-81981-6

Printed in the United States of America
Set in Old Style No. 7
Designed by Fritz A. Metsch

In memoriam,
Baroness Herta Riedl-Ursin

CONTENTS

Men frequently speak of space and time as if they were only concrete extent and duration, such as the individual consciousness can feel, but enfeebled by abstraction. In reality, they are representations of a wholly different sort, made out of other elements, according to a different plan, and with equally different ends in view.

—EMILE DURKHEIM

The Most
Beautiful House
in the World

(1)

WIND AND WATER

IT began with the dream of a boat. At a certain moment in my life (I was thirty-two), I was struck with what seemed an irresistible urge to become a sailor—or more accurately, to acquire a boat. This idiosyncrasy was not hereditary. There were no mariners in my background; my ancestral roots were in Red Ruthenia, several hundred miles from the Baltic. As far as I knew, my Polish forebears were sober, professional men, men of land, not water—not a Conrad among them. I don't want to give the impression that I wanted to run away to sea. I was no armchair Robert Louis Stevenson, I had no fantasy of sailing to the South Seas. Still, every boat dream has some suggestion of escape—in my case, escape from responsibilities, from the security of a university career, from the perils of everyday life.

My dream had another component, also shared by many of the thalassic fraternity (for this is predominantly a male fantasy)—not simply owning but *building* a boat. I ought to have known better. As a youngster I had seen plans of boats in *Popular Mechanics,* boats of such staggering simplicity that they could be built by "anyone with a hammer and saw"; and like many boys, I thought I would try my hand at it. The outcome was a tremendous case of sunburn, the result of an embarrassing afternoon spent drifting down a river on a windless day, sitting on a half-submerged, leaky hull so heavy that even the current had difficulty in moving it. It was an experience not to be repeated, which may be why, fifteen years later, it had become only a dim recollection instead of a discouragement.

Undeterred by memory, I read books on boatbuilding, wrote away for study plans and blueprints, and made lists of materials. After eight years of architectural education I was still only a passable carpenter, but I had become an accomplished model maker, and soon my study contained a small armada of cardboard sailing boats with masts made out of chopsticks, and billowing paper sails. A year passed. I had more or less settled on a design when I realized that I now had to find a place in which to build it. Finding such a space where I lived—in downtown Montreal—would not be easy. I had heard of a Hong Kong architect who was rebuilding an old Bugatti in an apartment, on the twelfth floor of a high-rise tower; but I was looking for a simpler solution. I needed a workshop for an extended period of time—judging from what I had read, several years was a not unreasonable estimate—which would be expensive. Several books suggested that the simplest and least expensive solution to this problem was to erect an impermanent wood-and-plastic shelter—a sort of greenhouse—which would last the necessary time and could then be easily taken down. I did know something about building construction, and for a young architect, even a boatshed represented a worthy challenge.

Or did it? Some people might question what business an

architect had designing a shed. Surely something this functional didn't require the talents of a professional! The common view is that architecture is something refined, something superfluous, that is added to plain buildings to make them "interesting." I once asked an engineer friend to advise me on the design of a structural system, and his first question was "Do you want something cheap or something architectural?" I knew that my boatbuilding shed had to be cheap, but I did want it "architectural" as well.

Nikolaus Pevsner began the introduction to his *Outline of European Architecture*—a book that was published the year I was born and has become a classic—with the following, often-quoted sentence: "A bicycle shed is a building; Lincoln Cathedral is a piece of architecture." In my twenty-five-year-old, well-thumbed paperback copy of Pevsner's book, the statement about the bicycle shed and the cathedral was underlined. As an architecture student, I had penciled a querulous question mark in the margin, so it must have disturbed me; it still did. I was not designing a bicycle shed, but I knew that my boatbuilding workshop was certainly out of the cathedral class. I was not sure that I liked the idea of my project being relegated to a distinctly inferior status, however. I had no quarrel about the significance of Gothic cathedrals—a visit to Chartres had been the architectural highlight of my postgraduation European grand tour—but I liked sheds too. Were the two really so different? What was it, exactly, that made a cathedral, and not a bicycle shed—or a boatshed—architecture?

Pevsner, an eminent art historian, suggested that architecture was distinguished from everyday building by being designed with a view to what he called aesthetic appeal.

"Aesthetic" means "sensitive to beauty." The cathedral is a work of consummate artistry, but who can say that the builder of a bicycle shed does not care about its appearance? He locates the supports symmetrically at each end; the woodwork is carefully jointed and planed; the roof is painted; ornamental trim is attached to the gable; a little carving is added to the brackets. What is the purpose of this additional effort if not "aesthetic appeal"?

Is it size that distinguishes architecture from humbler buildings? Cathedrals are more imposing than bicycle sheds. The tall nave of Lincoln towers seventy feet in the air, and stretches almost two hundred feet from the entrance to the crossing, and another two hundred and fifty feet beyond that into the vast Angel Choir. The columnar piers that reach to the apex of the ribbed vault recall a forest, and the darkness and chill are those of a huge cave. It is awe-inspiring.

On the basis of any number of massive piles of granite or marble, one is tempted to conclude that architecture must be monumental. But throughout the Renaissance and baroque periods, architects were often called upon to design chapels and garden pavilions. Brunelleschi's Pazzi Chapel in Florence, Bramante's tiny Tempietto of San Pietro in Rome, Palladio's family chapel at Maser, Ange-Jacques Gabriel's Petit Trianon at Versailles, and Josef Effner's delightful Pagodenburg in Munich: such little masterpieces readily find a place in the history books, suggesting that smallness is no obstacle to making the architectural grade.

All buildings have a function. They are undertaken not to gratify the designer but to fulfill a social purpose. Of course, compared with the high-minded role of a cathedral or of a chapel, the use of a shed is lowly indeed. This is what John Ruskin meant when he said that the purpose of architecture was to raise men's spirits, which "merely" utilitarian buildings were not required to do. But the impact of the cavernous Lincoln nave is not only because of the atmosphere of solemnity and worship, the smell of incense and the murmur of prayer, it is also the result of the manmade space itself. The giant Zeppelin hangars, built in Friedrichshafen in the early 1900s, must have had a comparable, breath-stopping effect. I had only examined photographs of these buildings, which were dismantled in 1918; but I did once visit the machine hall of LG 2, the great hydroelectric installation on the La Grande River in northern Quebec. This immense underground room—which is over sixteen hundred feet long and taller than Chartres Cathedral—made the same visceral impression on me. I felt small, and at the same time uplifted.

Is it sacrilegious to compare an airship hangar or a power station to a cathedral? Ruskin, who hated the "paltry art" of that great Victorian shed the Crystal Palace, would certainly have thought so. The famous art critic had cautioned his readers, "It is very necessary, in the outset of all inquiry, to distinguish carefully between Architecture and Building." The undisguised inference, later explained, was that only the former merited a refined person's attention. But I am not sure that the medieval cathedral builders would have objected. After all, some of the most magnificent structures they built were intended for mundane uses. Monastic cloisters, infirmaries, refectories, and even kitchens exhibited architectural pretensions no less monumental than those of the cathedral. When the secular canons of Lincoln needed a meeting place, they could have built a simple enclosure; instead, they constructed an extraordinary ten-sided chamber—the first polygonal chapter house in England. The ceiling, which was as tall as the nave of the adjoining cathedral, was supported on a single, soaring column, which fanned out at the top into a canopy of Purbeck marble vaulting. Light entered from all sides, through tall, stained-glass windows.

Important people, such as the canons of Lincoln, were powerful people. Like the monarchs, aristocrats, and business magnates who became the patrons of architects in later centuries, they wanted their buildings to express and commemorate this power, and to endure, and endure they did, outlasting their owners' time of supremacy and surviving for centuries.* Is architecture, then, simply buildings that manage to survive?

There is no doubt that our view of the past is a function of the available historical evidence. It is by the footprint that we know the foot. What is less obvious, as the historian Daniel J. Boorstin points out, is that the evidence according to which we know—or think we know—the past reflects a remarkably consistent bias. It is his thesis that the historical record is all too frequently not only incomplete but skewed: not exactly survival of the fittest but survival of the richest— of the immovable, the valuable, the durable, the collected and protected, and the academically classified.

Boorstin's Law has two effects. First, since historical knowledge is based on physical evidence, whatever survives assumes an importance which it may not originally have had. For example, the preponderance of existing Roman-

---

* Buildings must survive the ravages not only of time but also of fashion; until the nineteenth century, "Gothick" was a term of opprobrium, and medieval cathedrals were not admired by the architectural profession.

6

esque buildings in certain outlying regions of France has been used as evidence that it is here that the style originated. Bernard Berenson offers a different interpretation and suggests that places such as Cluny may have been simply too poor, or too indifferent, to refurbish their cathedrals in the more current Gothic style, which was the pattern in more prosperous communities, where the evidence of unadulterated Romanesque buildings is lacking. The Gothic cathedral endures as an artifact, but the religious attitudes of ordinary, feudal peasants are unrecorded; we can surmise that they may have been devout, but they could equally have been callous and superstitious in their attitude to the all-powerful Church. The corollary is also true: what does not survive remains outside the historical record. Indeed, as Boorstin suggests, the most everyday documents—the medieval shopping list or the ancient repair bill—are, precisely because of their ordinariness, the least likely to endure. This one-sided record can easily produce a distorted view of the past.

A future investigator of my own childhood, for example, could easily locate bureaucratic documents such as a birth certificate or my naturalization papers. Digging deeper, he would probably retrieve precious mementos such as a silver napkin ring (a christening gift "from Jean & Jimmy, Leven, 31/7/43") and a class medal ("Virtute et Labore"). He might unearth a yearbook showing an awkward thirteen-year-old posing stiffly with tousled hair and tie askew, and he might locate my report cards, or the program for the school play (*Billy Budd*) in which I am portentously identified as Set Manager. That is the official record. But he would not know what I did after I finished my homework. He would not discover the Lash LaRue comic books over which I pored

7

for hours, or my collection of *Popular Mechanics,* or my bird-watching lists—all long lost now. He would never find out about my beloved Dinky Toy tanks or about my lead soldiers. According to the surviving evidence, he would hardly know me.

So too with buildings. There is a wealth of official information about important monuments such as Lincoln Cathedral and about the men who built them. The original Lincoln nave was begun by Saint Hugh and was the work of Geoffrey de Noiers, although it is not clear whether this master mason was English or French. The beautiful chapter house was built during the episcopate of Hugh de Wells, a sensible man who also commissioned the kitchen and completed the hall of the bishop's palace. The bishop under whom the Angel Choir was commenced—it took twenty-four years to complete—was a man named Robert Grosseteste; the master mason was Simon Trask. It is generally assumed that patron and architect collaborated in many of the decisions, but eventually the master mason achieved individual prominence. The carving on the tomb of Hugues Libergier, a master mason of Reims, shows a man with a long cloak and staff—both badges of authority—and holding a model of the church of Saint-Niçaise. He has a possessive air.

But of the ordinary carvers and wrights who really built the cathedrals, little is known. Their homes—sheds, really— that surrounded the cathedral were constructed of inferior materials and have either disappeared or have undergone several hundred years of modification and change. Wattle-and-daub hovels do not last, and only recently have efforts been made to study such humble dwellings. Their illiterate builders have left us no record, and the few surviving buildings are mute. Who conceived the large English medieval stone barn that still stands at Great Coxwell, Berkshire? Even the date of this impressive building, which has marvelous timber vaulting and side aisles, is unknown— "erected at some time during the thirteenth century" is the best that the historians can do.

It would be convenient if architecture could be defined as any building designed by an architect. But who is an architect? Although the Académie Royale d'Architecture in Paris was founded in 1671, formal architectural schooling did not appear until the nineteenth century. The famous Ecole des Beaux-Arts was founded in 1816; the first English-language school, in London, in 1847; and the first North American university program, at MIT, was established in 1868. Despite the existence of professional schools, for a long time the relationship between schooling and practice remained ambiguous.* It is still possible to become an architect without a university degree, and in some countries, such as Switzerland, trained architects have no legal monopoly over construction. This is hardly surprising. For centuries, the difference between master masons, journeymen builders, joiners, dilettantes, gifted amateurs, and architects has been ill defined. The great Renaissance buildings, for example, were designed by a variety of non-architects: Brunelleschi was trained as a goldsmith, Mi-

---

* The two giants of late-nineteenth-century American architecture, Louis Sullivan and H. H. Richardson, both studied at the Beaux-Arts, but without completing the degree requirements. The great Victorian architect Edwin Lutyens studied at an art school for only two years, did not finish the course, and two years later established his practice, at the precocious age of twenty. Not one of the three best-known architects of the twentieth century—Frank Lloyd Wright, Ludwig Mies van der Rohe, and Le Corbusier—received a formal architectural education.

9

chelangelo as a sculptor, Leonardo da Vinci as a painter, and Alberti as a lawyer; only Bramante, who was also a painter, had formally studied building. These men are termed architects because, among other things, they created architecture—a tautology that explains nothing.

What the buildings that are illustrated in art-history books share is not uniformly trained creators but uniformly prominent patrons. It was the rich and famous who built the largest, the most expensive, the most impressive, and the most durable structures. And it was these structures—the cathedrals and the palaces—that were taken care of and eventually protected and restored. And these were the buildings that came to be studied, documented, and classified. Scholars usually belonged—or aspired to belong—to the ruling class, and naturally preferred to concern themselves with dignified and noble buildings; art historians left the study of mundane structures to archaeologists, anthropologists, and ethnographers. There was more than a little snobbism in this attitude, and it is hardly surprising that the recorded history of architecture became the history of a small group of selected buildings, an exclusive architectural winner's circle.

Outside the circle were what were condescendingly described as "vernacular" buildings. This term was borrowed from the study of language, where it referred to the native speech of a particular country or region; in an architectural context, it was often used to describe all nonpedigreed buildings. But as Eric Mercer, the author of a definitive study of traditional English farmhouses, suggests, what we call vernacular is merely whatever is common in a given area at a given time; the same building, in another time and place, might not be considered vernacular. In other words, so-called vernacular buildings—folk architecture—cannot be characterized by their inherent qualities but only by their shared commonness.

William Shakespeare ignored the difference between vernacular and "proper" English—and enriched the language immeasurably. All buildings—at least all buildings of a particular time and culture—share a vocabulary. In the case of Europe and America, the language of architecture has for centuries drawn its inspiration from classical antecedents. Instead of emphasizing the dissimilarities between grand and humble buildings, it is more useful to imagine a continuum, with prominent buildings for prominent purposes at one end and more ordinary buildings, for everyday functions, at the other.

The Galilee Porch of Lincoln Cathedral *is* a porch. It marks the entrance and provides shelter for the visitor— originally for the bishop, as this was a ceremonial doorway, opposite his palace. It performs the same function as the porch of a country cottage, although it is of course much grander, as befits a place of worship. The main door of the cathedral is located in the gable end of the nave, just like the door of the Great Coxwell barn. The timber roof of Lincoln also resembles those of medieval houses and barns, which were built by the same Anglo-Saxon wrights. Indeed, in many ways a cathedral resembles a great embellished barn, which is why the interior of a barn, with its tall posts and streaks of light, recalls the dignified gravity of a Gothic nave.*

---

* Am I exaggerating? Horace Walpole described Inigo Jones's Saint Paul's church in Covent Garden as the "handsomest barn in England," and, in a neat turn of history, one hundred and fifty years later, the architect James Playfair successfully used Saint Paul's as the model for an actual barn.

THE MOST BEAUTIFUL HOUSE

Architecture has been described as the art of building, but this is a judgment of effect rather than of cause. If we call buildings that move us "architecture," then we leave open the question of whether they are grand or small, known or unknown, sheds or cathedrals. And we leave open the question of who designed them. What finally distinguishes the members of the winner's circle from the uncouth mob of "mere" buildings is not their architectural quality but their social standing, the sanction of the critic and the art historian, and the effect of Boorstin's Law of Historical Survival, not any intrinsic attribute.

*   *   *

Before I could think about what my boatbuilding shed would look like, I needed a building site. City land was obviously too expensive; so, using a compass and taking Montreal as the center, I drew a circle on a map; the forty-five-mile radius represented one hour of driving time, the maximum distance I was willing to travel. During one summer my wife, Shirley, and I drove the perimeter of the circle. To the northwest, the Laurentian Mountains were attractive but long since occupied by vacation homes; we would have had to go farther than forty-five miles to find affordable land. To the north it was emptier, but the landscape was too untamed, too wild; I wanted to build a boat, not to become a pioneer. To the west it was too flat. We left south until last, which, under the circumstances, was a curious omission, since Lake Champlain, the only large body of water in the vicinity, was due south of Montreal. But maybe I had left south until last intentionally. Canadians go south to the Caribbean to avoid the winter cold, south to New York City to flee provincialism, and south over the border to avoid exorbitant liquor taxes and Sunday store closures. In Canada, south is the direction of escape; but I was not willing, at that point, to admit that this was what my boat dream was really about.

The local real-estate agent, at any rate, thought that he understood escape. He showed us what were optimistically called "mini-farms": parcels of uncultivated land that real farmers had long since abandoned—just the thing for urban homesteaders. Dismayed at our indifference, he suggested that there was one last place that we ought to see; an apple grower was selling off a corner of an old orchard, and maybe we would be interested.

It was October, and there were apples on the ground as we walked among the trees. What we saw as we emerged from the orchard was a long, flat meadow and beyond it a field, bounded on the far side by a hedgerow. When we reached the end of the meadow, where the flat land broke and started its gentle slope to the west, we stopped to admire the view. There was a prospect of land falling and rising and, in the distance, a low hill. I did not know then that the hill also deflected the westerly winter winds; for the moment, its comforting bulk anchored the entire landscape in place.

The ancient Chinese believed that in the features of the natural landscape one could glimpse the mathematically precise order of the universe and all the beneficial and harmful forces that were harmoniously connected according to the principle of the Tao—the Way. This was not a question of metaphor: the topography did not represent good or evil; it really *was* good or evil. Under these circumstances, locating a building in the landscape became a decision of momentous proportions that could affect an individual and his family for generations to come. The result was *feng-shui,* which means "wind and water," and which was a kind of cosmic surveying tool. Its coherent, scientific practice dates from the Sung dynasty (960–1126), but its roots are much older than that. It was first used to locate grave sites—the Chinese worshiped their ancestors, who, they believed, influenced the good fortune of their descendants. Eventually it began to be used to locate the homes of the living; and, indeed, the earliest book on *feng-shui,* published during the Han dynasty (202 B.C.–A.D. 220), was entitled *The Canon of the Dwellings.*

Feng-shui combined an intricate set of related variables that reflected the three great religions of China—Taoism, Buddhism, and Confucianism. First were the Taoist principles of yang and yin—male and female. The five Buddhist planets corresponded to the five elements, the five directions (north, south, west, east, and center), and the five seasons (the usual four and midsummer). *Feng-shui* employed the sixty-four hexagrams of the *I-Ching,* a classic manual of divination popularized by Confucius, and also made use of the astrological signs: the constellations were divided into four groups: the Azure Dragon (east), the Black Tortoise (north), the White Tiger (west), and the Red Bird (south).

The first task of the geomancer, who was called *feng-shui hsien sheng,* or "doctor of the vital force," was to detect the presence of each of these variables in the natural landscape. Hilly ground represented the Dragon; low ground was the Tiger: the ideal was to have the Dragon on the left and the Tiger on the right (hence, to face south). In a predominantly hilly area, however, a low spot was a good place to build; in flatter terrain, heights were considered lucky. The best site was the junction between the Dragon and the Tiger, which is why the imperial tombs around Beijing are so beautifully situated, just where the valley floor begins to turn into mountain slopes.

The shape of mountain peaks, the presence of boulders, and the direction of streams all incorporated meanings that had to be unraveled. Often, simple observation did not suffice, and the Chinese had to resort to external aids. The mariner's compass was a Chinese invention, but the *feng-shui* compass served a different purpose. It resembled a large, flat, circular platter. In the center, like the bull's-eye of a dart board, was a magnetic needle, surrounded by eighteen concentric circles. Each ring represented a different factor and was inscribed with the constellations, odd and even numbers, the planets and the elements, the seasons, the hexagrams, the signs of the zodiac, the solar orbit, and so on. With the aid of the compass, the geomancer could discover the existence of these variables even when they were not visible to the naked eye.

It might appear that *feng-shui* made man the victim of fate, but this was not the case. For one thing, there was a moral dimension to the belief; and to gain the full benefit of an auspiciously placed home, the family itself had to remain honest and upright. Moreover, the geomancer's job was not only to identify bad and good sites but also to advise on how to mitigate evil influences or to improve good ones. Trees could be planted to camouflage undesirable views; streams could be rerouted; mounds could be built up or cut down. It is no accident that the greatest Chinese art of all is gardening.

Many villages in China have a grove of trees or bamboo behind them, and a pond in front. The function of these picturesque features is not as landscaping embellishment, or at least it is not only that; they are intended to fend off evil influences. The pagodas that can still be seen built on the tops of hills and mounds serve the same purpose. When visiting some recently built farmhouses in the county of Wuqing, I noticed that the entrances to some of the courtyards were screened by a wall that forced the visitor to wind his way around it, as in a maze or an obstacle course. Such walls exist in other cultures; the Koran, for example, requires the entrances to all Islamic homes to be shielded by a wall. But the purpose of the *ying-pei,* as the Chinese walls are called, is not to prevent the passerby from looking in. These are "spirit walls" and are meant to keep out asomatous trespassers. The *ying-pei* is not an isolated superstition, like lucky horseshoes in the West; it too is a part of *feng-shui.*

No one was immune from the wind-and-water science, for all places had good or bad *feng-shui.* That of Hong Kong, for example, was generally considered to be particularly poor, because of the large numbers of rocks and boulders on the mountainsides.* During the nineteenth century, the British decided to locate their villas on the mountain slopes of Pok-Foo-Lum, on the northwest tip of the island. When they began laying out delicately curving roads, planting many trees, and even building a water reservoir, the Chinese were impressed, for these were exactly

---

* The inauspicious location of Hong Kong was no accident. According to one nineteenth-century missionary, "When land had to be ceded to the hated foreigner up and down the China Coast, as a so-called foreign concession, the Chinese Government would invariably select a spot condemned by the best experts in *feng-shui* as one that combined a deadly breath with all those indications of the compass which imply dire calamities upon all that settle down there and their children."

16

the precautions that *feng-shui* recommended as a protection against the malign breath that was said to permeate that place. They began to suspect that the foreigners were not as barbaric as they appeared.

It was unthinkable to the Chinese that anyone could be ignorant of something as powerful as *feng-shui*. Their own faith in it was unshakable, as the following story demonstrates. A farmer's house was attacked by robbers. His aged father and a relative were killed, and a servant wounded, although the robbers were driven off and nothing was stolen. When the farmer was asked why he did not move to the safety of a nearby town, he replied that it would be foolish to do so, since the *feng-shui* of this place was so good that anyone living there was bound to prosper. This incident was recounted by a Baptist missionary in 1923.

The European and American missionaries who worked in China during the nineteenth century had been extremely critical of what they considered to be a crude, pagan superstition and an impediment to Christianity. The Reverend Ernest John Eitel, a clergyman of the London Missionary Society, published what is still one of the few scholarly books in English on *feng-shui* but was unable to find much of value in what he called "a farrago of nonsense and childish absurdities." The Reverend J. Edkins, writing in the *Chinese Recorder and Missionary Journal,* called the belief "one of the great obstacles to civilization." Such statements were not founded in ignorance—both Eitel and Edkins were scrupulous and thorough in their descriptions—but in their recognition of the high regard that all Chinese had for the wind-and-water science. *Feng-shui* created many problems for missionaries and modernizers alike. A visitor to any traditional Chinese neighborhood will remark at the uniform low height of all the buildings. *Feng-shui* prevented any single house from acquiring undue influence over its neighbors by being higher; one can imagine the consternation caused by the overpowering yang of tall mission-church steeples. According to *feng-shui,* long, straight lines in the landscape, whether mountain ridges or rivers, were especially unlucky; hence the sinuous forms and tortuous features of Chinese gardens. Canals, railways, and telegraph lines inevitably came into conflict with this criterion and more often than not had to be rerouted. Indeed, it is thanks to their strong *feng-shui* that the beautiful valleys containing the Ming and the Qing tombs are unmarred by highways, transmission lines, or railway tracks.

By 1920, it appeared to Lucius Chapin Porter, a young missionary and Peking University professor who was born in China and was sympathetic to Chinese culture, that "without question, the pseudo-science of Feng Shui will pass away—indeed, it is already passing." This view was mistaken—it was the work of the missionaries that would pass away, not *feng-shui.* Nor did geomancy prove to be as incompatible with modernization as the foreigners foretold. The headquarters of the Hongkong and Shanghai Banking Corporation—recently built at a reputed $1 billion construction cost—is the most expensive and technologically advanced skyscraper in the world. A visitor might wonder about the odd angle of the escalators that lead from the plaza to the main banking floor; instead of following the rigidly orthogonal geometry of the rest of the building, they are placed at a distinctly odd angle, almost as if by accident. Their orientation was not determined by the vagaries of architectural fashion, however, or by a traffic expert, but by another kind of consultant, Lung King Chuen. Lung, a forty-eight-year-old man whose newspaper photograph could be that of a stockbroker, is a *feng-shui* master. He also advised the British architects of the building that the giant cross-bracing that they had made the main feature of the banking hall was an extremely unfortunate choice: according to *feng-shui,* the X-shape is not harmonious and is a bad omen. He recommended that bamboo be planted in front of the offending elements; it would grow quickly and obscure the unlucky sign. The architects modified the interior accordingly.

Across the street from the Hongkong Bank is the building site of the future headquarters of the Bank of China, a seventy-story building whose extremely tall structure requires more than the usual amount of wind bracing. The American architects incorporated these great trusses into the design of the façade, producing a characteristic pattern of X's. *Feng-shui* once again intervened, although this time it was the client who expressed concern about such negative symbolism on his bank. The design was changed, and with a bit of camouflage, the X's were converted to triangular shapes. The change did not please everyone; Sung Siu-kwong, who hosts a weekly *feng-shui* television show, claimed that "triangles mean danger. Not too many people like them, except the Egyptians." What was remarkable about this controversy was not only the durability of the belief in the wind-and-water science but the client involved: he was not Taoist but Maoist—the bank is owned and operated by the People's Republic of China.

Feng-shui continues to be used widely in Hong Kong and surreptitiously in mainland China, although the regime there has declared it illegal, at least for local consumption. That is curious, since *feng-shui* has always ignored wealth and social rank; it has determined orientation and placement and identified the particular spiritual characteristics of a site, both for the grave of a simple peasant and for the tombs of the emperor's family and retinue. The same spirit walls that I observed in simple farmhouses I also saw in the Forbidden City in Beijing, shielding the entrance to the living quarters of the last empress and protecting her from *sha-ch'i*—the death spirit—a spirit that apparently drew no distinction between palaces and sheds.

ᏋᏋ ᏋᏋ ᏋᏋ

The real-estate agent pointed out the boundary lines of the orchard and the meadow to us. A *feng-shui* doctor would have commented on the favorable topography. There was the Azure Dragon on the left (a bluff to the east) and the White Tiger on the right (undulating, low ground to the west); to the south was running water (a stream), also an auspicious sign. The gentle landscape exhibited a reticence that was much favored by the ancient Chinese. But I understood all this only later; for the moment it seemed merely a particularly comfortable spot. Shirley and I looked at each other and knew that we had found the place.

We were standing at the boundary between two meadows. What had drawn us here was a single, twisted tree—a renegade apple from the orchard. Trees have always been full of symbolism. For Hindus, neem trees are objects of worship; Christians bring an evergreen into their homes at Christmastime; and majestic oaks are often given pride of place in English country estates. Trees form social spaces, shady canopies beneath which people like to congregate; hence the location of trees with respect to buildings is of the utmost importance, though in this case it was the other way around: the old apple tree had been here for several decades—we had only just arrived.

(2)

••

THE BUILDING GAME

A T the time that I acquired the land for my boatbuilding
workshop, I had a small architectural practice, although "practice" was too grand a word for my modest
commissions. Or it may have been accurate, for I *was* practicing—that is, learning. The projects were usually small
homes for young families with limited budgets—a difficult
combination, for a small house is not easier to design than
a large one, and an inexpensive cottage is in some ways a
greater challenge than a mansion.

I particularly remember one case, a house for a young
engineer and his family with many requirements and not
much money. Where would the bookshelves go in the living
room? Could we fit a sauna in somewhere? Could they have
a greenhouse, even a small one? Jacqueline wanted a sewing
room; her husband required a study, or at least a quiet place
for a desk; the children needed space to play. I needed to
fit all this into less than twelve hundred square feet or we
would exceed our budget.

We had many meetings—negotiations, really—to discuss
their future home. It was after one long evening, as we sat
around the kitchen table, strewn with notes and sketches,

that Jim told me, "I never realized before what it was that an architect really did."

I was startled by this statement; but, on reflection, it was not surprising that architecture has remained for many a mysterious profession. We see doctors and dentists regularly, accountants once a year; and sooner or later the pinstriped practitioners of the law enter our lives. But even if we have little personal contact with these professionals, even if we are healthy and law-abiding and file our own tax returns, we know—or we think we know—the work that they do. Lawyers and doctors have written about their occupations, and they have been written about, and television dramas have informed us of the intimate details of the operating room and the law office.

How has Hollywood depicted the drafting room? In *The Girl in the Red Velvet Swing,* made in 1955, Ray Milland portrayed Stanford White, the celebrated architect who designed many New York City landmarks. But it was not his professional accomplishments that attracted Twentieth Century–Fox. White was unusually talented, but he was also rich and glamorous, and a socialite, and his life was touched by scandal—he was murdered, in 1906, by the husband of his mistress, the girl in the swing. This forgettable movie remains, as far as I know, the only filmed biography of an architect. A decorous practitioner like H. H. Richardson, who was a more influential architect and for whom White worked as a young man, was never memorialized on the screen. Nor was that peripatetic genius Frank Lloyd Wright, although his long life was sufficiently melodramatic and was said to have influenced Ayn Rand's novel *The Fountainhead.* King Vidor turned this turgid architectural allegory into a movie; but since its climax shows the overwrought hero blowing up one of his own buildings, it can hardly be said to have enlightened the public about what architects really do.

The word "architect," which in one guise or another is common to all the modern European languages, is derived from the ancient Greek. Just as an archbishop is the head bishop, the *architekton* was the chief *tekton*, which is to say he was the chief carpenter. The Sanskrit word for architect, *sthapati*, as well as the Mandarin *chientsu-shu*, also means "master builder." They all suggest that what architects "do" is to build. But if I were to ask my architecture students what they do for untold hours, daytime and nighttime, as they work on their assignments, they would not answer that they were learning how to build; they would say, "We are designing." What does that mean? The place where the students work is called a design studio, which implies that this is a creative activity; but what goes on there would puzzle the casual visitor. To begin with, the room is completely unlike the well-kept scientific laboratories and orderly engineering workshops elsewhere in the university—and unlike most people's idea of an artist's studio. The design studio recalls a medieval town—or rather a Calcutta *bustee,* for it is subdivided into many small workplaces and cubicles by improvised partitions of cloth, cardboard, and plywood, and the narrow aisles between them form a maze of lanes and dead-end alleys. There are drawing tables, to be sure; after all, the meaning of the Italian *disegnare* was "to trace out or draw" (a French draftsman is still called a *dessinateur*), and dexterity with a pencil has long been considered an indispensable architectural skill. There are sheets pinned to the walls—the room is awash in paper, to the despair of the cleaning staff. There are meticulously inked drawings, but also watercolors, charcoal illustrations, photographs, silk screens, collages, even finger paintings.

But this is not only a drawing room. Scattered around the studio are a variety of materials: paper, cardboard, modeling clay, twigs, polystyrene, and plaster of paris. These are used to build the models that can be seen in various stages of completion. A metropolis of cardboard and acetate office buildings is laid out on a worktable for the teacher's scrutiny; the pell-mell urban landscape resembles Houston or Dallas. A few feet away the geography changes, and country homes are set in forests of lichen, next to glass lakes dotted with paper sailboats. There are balsa-wood frame houses, with siding removed to expose cotton-batting insulation. There are rooms with little chairs and rugs, and entire city blocks with parks and streetlights, lines of plastic cars, and crowds of matchstick people.

Writers write, painters paint, and sculptors sculpt. Nothing comes between them and their medium. Composers make abstract signs that symbolize music, but they can at least whistle the melody. But when the architect creates, it is always at one step removed. He builds, but not on the building site, not with bricks and mortar but with card and balsa wood, with modeling clay and wood blocks, in a make-believe universe of people three-quarters of an inch high.

I have noticed that visitors to the design studio, or to an architect's office, are unfailingly drawn to these models. They stoop down and peer in, enchanted by the ingenious miniature replicas. Our fascination with smallness is something very old; excavations of ancient sites frequently unearth figurines and tiny facsimiles of military and domestic objects. Miniature replicas of household objects resurfaced in the nineteenth century, although not in the coffin but on the mantelpiece. Such knickknacks are still common. Earlier, during the seventeenth century, cupboards that opened to reveal intricate and expensive house interiors, the rooms furnished with tiny chandeliers and postage-stamp paintings, had been fashionable in Germany and Holland. The crèche beneath the Christmas tree is an Italian custom that has survived to the present day. Trading companies exhibited models of their clipper ships in glass cases, as maritime shippers and airlines continue to do. Yacht owners hang half-hull models on the wall; like the architectural models that stand in office-building lobbies, these miniatures have a talismanic, protective function. There is something magical about these little worlds.

There is something else that makes architectural models so appealing, and so familiar: the tiny buildings peopled with pocket-size figures recall the doll's houses and lead soldiers of our childhood. We have all spent hours sprawled on the floor playing with toy blocks and built little houses with Lego bricks or some other construction toy. We have all been little architects.

≈   ≈   ≈

There are so many examples of construction toys of one sort or another that one might assume that this is an immemorial game of childhood. Archaeologists have discovered a variety of miniature objects: Sumerian pull-along chariots, Egyptian board games, Chinese kites, Greek rattles, Mesopotamian clay goats and bulls, Roman bronze soldiers. Whether these were really toys is not always clear, since many of the small animals and personages have been found in tombs and probably had funerary, not recreational, uses. And even in those cases where they were playthings, it is by no means apparent that they were associated with children. Whether these were toys or talismans, one thing is certain: none of them even remotely resembles a construction game.

Pieter Brueghel the Elder's painting *Children's Games,* dated 1560, is an encyclopedic depiction of a large variety of toys, games, and play pastimes—art historians have counted as many as ninety-one distinct games on the crowded canvas. We can recognize blindman's buff, leap-frog, and hide-and-seek, as well as hockey, skittles, blowing soap bubbles, and ball playing. Almost all the games that Brueghel painted are still played, four hundred years later. One little rascal—a Flemish Tom Mix—leans out of a window pointing a pop gun. There are many toys—dolls, jacks, hoops, spinning tops, as well as that favorite Low Country game, marbles. In some cases, real objects have been temporarily appropriated for play: a girl balances a broom, two boys rock on a barrel. In the foreground there are some bricks—real bricks—that have been halfheartedly placed in a semicircle, and abandoned. This is as close as we come to a building game.

In seventeenth-century Holland, artists and writers were fascinated by children's games, which they made the subject of many paintings and books; indeed, the Dutch are said to have invented this genre. They have left us with detailed inventories of games and toys, which have been exhaustively studied by modern scholars. Kites, stilts, skipping ropes, whirligigs, hobbyhorses, hoops, soap bubbles, dolls, and marbles were popular, as they had been for centuries. Golf and bowling achieved a prominence that they had not enjoyed before, and were played by both adults and children. But there was still no evidence of anything resembling a construction toy.

Philippe Ariès has demonstrated that during the Middle Ages and as late as the eighteenth century, young and old played the same games. That is to say, the distinction between the two was blurred; adults played games that we would consider childish (blindman's buff, leapfrog, hide-and-seek), and very young children engaged in such "grown-up" pastimes as gambling, fencing, and tennis. There was a similar ambiguity regarding toys, or what we now call toys, for the word did not acquire its modern meaning until the end of the sixteenth century. Children's playthings were sometimes scaled-down versions of real objects—little drums, or hobbyhorses—but most toys originated not with children but with adults. In Elizabethan England puppet shows were adult amusements, and remained so for a long time—Punch and Judy entertained Dr. Johnson and Jonathan Swift. During the reign of Henri IV, French courtiers annoyed passersby with peashooters. Eighteenth-century Parisians—grown-ups, not children—played with *pantins,* or jumping jacks, and with the *bilboquet,* or cup and ball; it was only after these fads passed that the playthings were appropriated by children. Diabolo—a Chinese toy consisting of a wooden reel balanced on a string stretched between two sticks—was introduced in 1764 to London, where it became an adult craze, as it did in Paris fifty years later. Even when adult playthings were taken up by children, that did not always mean that they were considered solely as children's toys: adults continued to play with jacks and knucklebones until well into the eighteenth century. If most toys were really hand-me-downs, and since grown-ups did not play with building blocks, where were construction toys to come from?

The fondness of children for traditional games is apparent if one examines the paintings of an eighteenth-century French artist such as Jean-Baptiste Siméon Chardin. Chardin was a master of the domestic genre, and in his paintings of children—two hundred years later and in another country—the games of Brueghel recur: throwing knucklebones, blowing soap bubbles, spinning tops. In several paintings he depicted a young boy playing with cards. Cards had been known in Europe for hundreds of years, and card-playing was a favorite activity of young and old—there are several seventeenth-century allegorical Dutch paintings of children playing cards. What is novel is the game that Chardin has portrayed—the boy is building a *château de cartes,* a house of cards. Children have finally begun to play the building game.

The origins of using playing cards as construction toys are obscure, but building with cards seems to have been well established when Chardin chose it as the theme of six paintings, done between 1735 and 1741.* Jean de La Bruyère mentioned it in *Les caractères,* which was published in 1688, and Milton referred to the frailty of a "house built of Court-cards" as early as 1641; both writers used the house of cards as a metaphor for instability and impermanence, as we still do today. What is striking is that all the early

---

* There are earlier depictions of this game: François Boucher produced an engraving of a young girl building a house of cards, and Nicolas Lancret's *L'Air* showed two adolescents, a boy and a girl, in the same activity. The oldest example I have come across is by Charles-Antoine Coypel, who was director of the Academy of Painting and Louis XV's painter; he portrayed two children building a house of cards in 1725.

references make it clear that this game was played exclusively by children. If that is true, and considering the improvised nature of using playing cards in this fashion, then this was one of the first toys that originated in children's (not adults') play, and it may even have been "invented" by them.

There is one reason the construction toy should have appeared so late. In an obscure monograph on building games, H. G. Wells wrote that "the jolliest indoor games for boys and girls demand a floor, and the home that has no floor upon which games may be played falls so far short of happiness." The house of Brueghel's day had a floor, of course, but it was a very busy floor. Rooms were not differentiated according to function, and cooking, eating, working, entertaining, and sleeping coexisted in the same space, in bustling intimacy. There was little provision for quiet or solitary activities. Children did not have their own bedrooms, let alone nurseries, and their play occurred out of doors—usually, as in *Children's Games,* in the street. This was hardly a suitable place for something as delicate as a house of cards. The street remained the locale for children's play until the mid-seventeenth century, when attitudes toward children began to change, and the smaller, and more intimate, family home made its appearance. After that, children who played in public were called urchins, guttersnipes, or street arabs—which were all eighteenth-century terms of disapproval.

Proper children, like those of Chardin's friends, played indoors, at home. His painting, *The Son of M. Lenoir Playing at Making a House of Cards,* shows a young boy, eight or nine years old, dressed in a frock coat and tricorne hat, leaning over a green-baize-covered gaming table. He is so intent on adding a playing card to his little construction that he pays us no attention whatsoever. Art historians have pointed out that Chardin was the first painter to capture the innocent absorption of children's play, and that this quality was absent in earlier depictions of childhood. The sweet calm of this solitary child is in sharp contrast to the frenetic activity of Brueghel's crowded playground or to the jolly gaiety of Dirk Hals's wide-eyed gamins. But it does not detract from Chardin's genius to suggest that it was also the nature of play itself that had changed.

Outdoor public play had been convivial; to play meant to play with others. So it was that most early games—hopscotch, hide-and-seek, leapfrog—were group games. But already in seventeenth-century Holland, where domesticity developed first, we see children playing in the home, alone. When play moved indoors, it not only became more private, it changed its disposition. It became, so to speak, domesticated. Outdoor games were boisterous, noisy, and usually rowdy; they still are. It takes long periods of quiet concentration to build a house of cards, and the availability of this time signals the growing isolation and introspection of children's play. Not surprisingly, this was the period when many indoor toys made their appearance: lead soldiers, clockwork toys, jigsaw puzzles, and dolls' houses.* There were also a variety of domestic card games. The French pastime (*passe-temps*) solitaire became popular in England during the eighteenth century; and although it was played by adults, it was considered a children's game.

In eighteenth-century painting, the activity of building

---

* The famous Dutch house cabinets, or *puppenhuizen,* of the seventeenth century had not been intended for play. The fashion for giving dolls' houses—they were called baby houses—to children began in England in the early 1700s.

an insubstantial house of cards, like blowing soap bubbles or spinning a top, had a secondary, moral meaning, and was intended as a "vanity image." In the tradition of the seventeenth-century Dutch painters, whom he admired, Chardin included a veiled reference to the frivolousness of such youthful games by producing a pair of contrasting paintings: the pendant to *House of Cards* is a paragon of industriousness titled *The Young Schoolmistress*. This artistic conceit undoubtedly reflected a widely held view regarding such games, and the house of cards could be said to represent the playful side of the family in the genealogy of the construction toy. There is another, more serious side.

I remember that when I built houses of cards I was forbidden to bend or fold them, since this would have spoiled them for my parents' bridge evenings. It was a hard temptation to resist, since it would have added greatly to the stability of my little structures. In Chardin's painting, the young M. Lenoir has folded several of the cards, which suggests that they were used exclusively for his game and, as sometimes happened to me, that he had been given an old deck. It was a small step from this to producing special cards for children's play. There was a long tradition of producing picture cards for children: illustrated playing cards had been used for teaching history and geography ever since the seventeenth century. These were the antecedents of instructional building cards, printed with pictures of birds and animals and letters of the alphabet, and with interlocking notches cut out at one end, to make the house of cards physically, as well as pedagogically, more solid. By the early 1800s, we encounter picture cards illustrated with parts of houses—doors and windows—that lent an air of even greater reality to the final construction.

The nineteenth century's interest in educational toys was

typified by the German teacher Friedrich Froebel, the pioneer of the kindergarten movement. An important ingredient of the "Froebel system" was the role of play—games, songs, and toys—in the creative development of the young child. In 1837, Froebel introduced what he called the Nine Gifts, a series of play materials of increasing complexity, to which the kindergarten child was sequentially exposed. The first three gifts consisted of a soft ball, wooden spheres, and cubes that could be assembled into various abstract geometrical shapes. The fourth gift was called "building bricks," and was intended for making miniature "forms of life"—that is, little household objects and little houses. "House and room, table and bench, are usually the first things the child represents, and he likes the former best, opened with doors and windows," Froebel wrote. He composed a song to accompany this activity:

> A house, a house, a house!
> A house belongs to me.
> A house, a house, a house!
> Come here, come here and see!

It is not clear if Froebel's were the first building blocks, but I have not come across any earlier examples.

In *The Cricket on the Hearth,* written in 1845, Charles Dickens described a toy merchant's workroom and its contents. The thirty-three-year-old author, who at this time had a large and growing family, would have been something of an expert on toys. He described dolls and dolls' houses, Noah's arks filled with animals, hobbyhorses and jumping jacks and musical carts—he even mentioned the popular Victorian magic lantern—but no building blocks. Of course, he could hardly have known of Froebel's work, since the first Froebelian kindergarten was established in England nine years later. But before that happened, and perhaps influenced by the Nine Gifts, German companies began manufacturing wooden play blocks for children.

Throughout the nineteenth century new toys arrived as fads, just as they do today, and when play blocks did become popular, they spread quickly. By the 1850s, the term "building blocks" was coming into common use. In keeping with their perceived educational function, these blocks, which were usually made of wood, were inscribed or lithographed with pictures of animals, numbers, and commonly with letters. In 1876, Thomas Eakins painted his two-year-old niece intently building a little arch with alphabet blocks. By then other variations of the construction toy were available. The British "New Alphabet Game" included wedge-shaped blocks that could be used to form a circular building. "Crandall's ABC Building Slabs" were made in New York in 1867 and consisted of flat wooden card-shaped pieces, one inch by two inches, illustrated with letters, and with dovetails on two edges so that they could be slotted together. In short order, the idea of standardized, interlocking pieces would lead to full-fledged construction kits.

The British construction toy Meccano was invented by Frank Hornby (who went on to make clockwork trains and the famous Dinky Toys) in 1901; A. C. Gilbert began manufacturing the Erector set—an American derivative—in 1920. The original Lincoln Logs were also patented in 1920, and log kits quickly became popular and are still being produced. The reason that Lincoln Logs and Erector sets seem quaint today is that they were made out of real building materials—wood and steel. Before plastic overwhelmed

33

toy manufacturing, this was not unusual. A late-nineteenth-century German manufacturer, Richters, sold tiny building bricks made out of cast cement—"Beware of quicklime imitations," warned the label. In 1918, A. E. Lott, in England, began making building sets that were cut from Italian marble. What a pleasure they must have been to handle! Lott's game, which was endorsed by Queen Mary, was an early example of astute marketing—parents were encouraged to buy additional components to expand the set, which was intended to last, generations if need be. This was also the case with a later construction toy such as Lego. Lego is a relative newcomer—it was invented in Denmark in 1949 —but it has become the most durably and universally popular toy in the modern world. There are said to be sixty-eight million children in one hundred and twenty-five countries playing with the tiny interlocking plastic bricks.

Not surprisingly, several of these construction toys were conceived by architects, or would-be architects: Froebel, arguably the inventor of building blocks, had intended to be an architect, and at twenty-three he had already begun his apprenticeship when a friend convinced him to become a teacher in a progressive school instead. The inventor of Lego, Ole Kirk Christiansen, was a joiner, and hence a *tekton*. His son Godtfred, who expanded the company after his father's death, certainly qualifies as an *architekton*—his Legoland amusement park includes a facsimile of the entire port of Copenhagen, built out of three million Lego bricks. A. E. Lott sought the advice of an architect, Arnold Mitchell, when he started producing his marble bricks; and Lincoln Logs were invented by John Lloyd Wright, the son of the famous architect.

Perhaps because my father was an engineer, I had an

assortment of construction toys. They varied in complexity. Meccano (I was raised in England) provided strips of metal, pierced with evenly spaced holes, that could be joined together with nuts and bolts to make towers, bridges, and machines. Another toy, whose name I no longer remember, was more architectural: it consisted of a base with a grid of holes into which one could place little metal rods. A variety of grooved plastic panels could be slid down between the rods to form walls. The solid panels, stamped with brick patterns, were red and white, the doors and window frames were green; the style was postwar contemporary, although there were delicately curved bow windows and hipped, tiled roofs. Simpler, and certainly more durable (the soft metal rods were always getting bent), was my box of Canadian Logs—a Commonwealth variant of Wright's invention— little cedar dowels of different lengths, notched at the corners so that they could be stacked up in imitation of traditional log construction.

I thought of my own play logs when, twenty years later, I built a summer house out of full-size, machined, interlocking, cedar logs which came from British Columbia, not in a box but in a boxcar—Canadian Logs, indeed. It is always tempting to make a direct link between the play of the child and the work of the adult; there was a mid-nineteenth-century French building toy called "Le petit architecte." None other than Frank Lloyd Wright himself recounted in his autobiography that he had played with Froebel blocks and that these had had an important influence on his creative development. The Los Angeles architect Frank Gehry has claimed that his choice of career was influenced by his childhood construction play, and several of his projects do have the air of large playthings. As a

35

young graduate I worked for Moshe Safdie, the architect of Montreal's Habitat, which has often been likened to a pile of children's play blocks and was in fact designed using Lego bricks; one of Safdie's later projects, a student union in San Francisco, resembled a house of cards. Buildings in the style known as High Tech often look like giant Erector sets. The neoclassical designs of postmodern architects, who celebrate engineering not at all, have a Froebelian, toylike quality, as if they were made of wooden blocks—colored cubes, cylinders, and pyramids.

It is safe to say that most modern children have played with construction toys of one sort or another, so one should not make too much of the causal relationship. Nevertheless, there is an affinity between construction toys and the grown-up world of architecture. I have often been struck by how much the disorganized and chaotic atmosphere of the design studio resembles that of a children's nursery. For a long time it puzzled me why this should be so. It was not because the students were childish, for they took their work seriously, and not because they lacked discipline. Perhaps it was their little cubicles, which resembled a child's improvised playhouse and made me feel a little like an adult interloper, or the motley drawings pinned up on the walls. Or was it because the basis of their work was "Let's pretend"? What they did was real enough, and yet the miniature worlds in whose making they were so totally absorbed were imagined.

      ❧   ❧   ❧

The wise Dutch historian J. H. Huizinga studied the nature and significance of play as an element of culture and suggested that it had three main characteristics. First, play was voluntary; second, it was not "ordinary," it involved a temporary pretense; and third, it was self-contained. These attributes can be easily recognized in children's games such as hide-and-seek, and in adult pastimes such as tennis; but Huizinga argued further that rites and rituals—profane and sacred—and many other spheres of human culture incorporated play characteristics. If the theater and the church contain play elements (and Huizinga's aim was not to trivialize religion—far from it), then why not the architect's studio?*

All games are based on conformity to rules, and the architect plays the building game according to two main conventions: one has to do with cutting, the other with magnification. The designer slices through reality—a horizontal cut produces the plan, a vertical one the cross section, a slice just in front of the wall produces a façade. A set of architect's construction drawings contains only these three slices or, rather, variations of them. That is part of the game—where to make the cut. The other part has to do with magnification—how close, or how far away, do we want to be from what we are looking at? In my own case, I could make a drawing of the entire plot of land so that the workshop appeared as a minute rectangle; or I could slice through the foundation footing and represent the reinforcing bars as thick as pencils, and distinguish every piece of gravel. Whatever I chose, the architect's scale reduced

---

* I must admit that Huizinga himself did not consider that the plastic arts, including architecture, contained the play element to any marked degree. It is true that buildings, unlike music or dance, are immobile and that the experience of architecture is difficult to interpret as play. But the *making* of buildings—their practicality notwithstanding—is much more playful than he imagined.

all reality to neat, comprehensible shapes. It was in this sense that design was play; for, like play, it not only created order, it *was* order.

One of the rules that I imposed on myself was to avoid complexity in plan, since odd shapes are difficult to roof, and the more corners a building has, the more difficult, and expensive, it is to build. This is why simple, one-room shelters such as wigwams, yurts, and igloos have often been circular—no corners at all. But a circular building was hardly suited to building a boat, so in my case the rules dictated a building that could be either square or rectangular. On the other hand, my building game had no rules about the construction material, and this changed from plastic, to cement block, (briefly) to compacted earth, to wood, back to cement block, and back again to wood. Roof shapes could likewise be altered. Plastic can be made to curve; with modern materials flat roofs are just as practical as sloped ones, even in the Canadian climate; and with a different covering, the pitch of an angled roof can be low or steep, as the designer wishes. This too became a game. A colleague of mine once derisively referred to "putting hats on buildings," suggesting that architectural design should take itself more seriously. But I did feel like a person in a hat shop: which to choose—the practical wool watch cap, the floppy beret, the broad-brimmed Stetson, or the imposing topper?

The psychologist Bruno Bettelheim once described children's play as an activity "characterized by freedom from all but personally imposed rules (which are changed at will), by free-wheeling fantasy involvement, and by the absence of any goals outside the activity itself." This is a very good description of the designer at his drafting table. "In architecture, Palladio is the game!!" wrote Edwin Lutyens in a letter to a colleague. His choice of word was deliberate, for he viewed tradition not as a constraint but as an opportunity, and his buildings were characterized by self-conscious manipulation of the rules, and even by frivolity, although these were always contained within the playing field of classicism.

Bettelheim quotes a four-year-old who asks, "Is this a fun game or a winning game?" The solitary building game is definitely a fun game—there is no opponent. The concept of fun is elusive and resists easy definition, but it is an undisputed element—perhaps *the* element—of play.* In the present context, it is enough to note that fun does not imply folly, or any lack of seriousness—quite the opposite. To say that design is fun goes a long way toward explaining the continued attraction of a profession that is characterized by relatively low pay and far from secure employment. It also explains the intense absorption of the architecture student, the countless hours spent at the drawing table, the long nights. What keeps him involved for such long periods of time is that the outcome of the design process is unpredictable: it is the result of chance, as in play. He does not know ahead of time exactly what the result will be. He could save himself a lot of time and look for a similar building to reproduce exactly; but this would make as little sense as building the same house of cards over and over again, or solving the same crossword puzzle. The issue here is not only originality but fun.

---

* Huizinga pointed out the curious anomaly that no modern language that he knew had an exact equivalent of the English "fun." The Québecois vernacular has made up for this lack by borrowing the English word, hence, "C'est le fun."

Huizinga wrote that play "marks itself off from the course of the natural process. It is something added thereto and spread out over it like a flowering, an ornament, a garment . . . [it is] a stepping out of 'real' life into a temporary sphere of activity with a disposition all of its own." Bettelheim also mentions fantasy involvement as an ingredient of play. Indeed, much of the work of design goes on in the imagination. I do not mean inspiration but rather the act of imagining, playing "Let's pretend." The attraction of that children's game for me was that it needed no justification—I could be anything I wanted: a ghost, a cowboy, a pirate. Le Corbusier's improbable question "Why shouldn't a house look like a ship?" had a similar insouciance. His answer was the Villa Savoye, a country house that pretended to be the superstructure of an ocean liner, sailing, or at least floating (since it was raised on posts) on a lawn. There were funnel shapes on the roof, and the garden was not on the ground but in the air; from a second-floor terrace, the inhabitants— that is, the passengers—experienced the surrounding landscape as if from a ship's deck.

On a more prosaic level, the designer tries to imagine how the building will look when it is finished; and, more important, he tries to imagine himself inside the finished building. These are the sorts of questions that architecture students are often asked in class: "Take me through your design." "How do I come in?" "What do I do first?" "Where do I sit down to take off my overshoes?" "Where do I hang my coat?" And it can be more complicated: "If it's raining, do I get wet fumbling for my keys?" or "If I am inside, can I see who's coming to the door?" or "How do I get out of the bedroom in case of fire?"

Building a house of cards starts easily enough, just two

cards leaning one against the other; but as the house grows and the cards totter and need support—soon it is the game that leads the player. So also in design, ideas collapse and have to be rebuilt; one thing suggests another, and the architect hurries to catch up.* At the same time, rules can be changed, and the freedom to modify rules is something that both design and solitary play have in common. This was reflected in my own sketches of the boatbuilding workshop, which sometimes represented the plan, sometimes the cross section, sometimes an exterior view, and sometimes a detail of construction. It was a graphic record of an inner conversation. If the roof was shaped like this, it had to be built a certain way. But that made it difficult to connect the roof to the walls—also it looked ugly. If I changed the width of the building, however, the roof angle could be less steep— at this point the solar heater would probably have to be abandoned, but other things were falling into place, and at least some heat from the sun would come through the rooflight. And what if the wide doors were glazed, and moved from the end of the building to one of the side walls, facing south? It was at that point that I must have remembered why the doors were there, for the next sketches show the ghostly outline of the boat, rotating and sliding out of the opening. I worked for hours at a time, no less absorbed in my little world than Chardin's solitary boy in his.

---

* Note how different this process is from the popular misconception that the architect envisages the building whole, in his mind's eye. The hastily scrawled sketch—the napkin plan of architectural legend—is often reproduced in monographs on prominent architects. I have always suspected that such sketches, which are intended as a proof of inspirational genius, have been chosen with hindsight, from among dozens of discarded drawings.

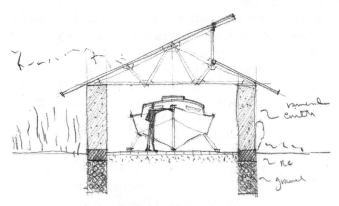

A BOATBUILDING SHED

This raises the third characteristic of play: that it is self-contained, and comprises its own course and meaning. The goal of play is play itself. There are no loose ends in play, none of the indeterminacy that characterizes ordinary life. We feel in control. There is something very pleasant about the limitedness of play; it gives games such as tennis or golf the familiarity of liturgy. Games take place within fixed boundaries of space and time: the court, the playground, the card table. Architecture takes place in a broad and worldly context, of course; but the building game is played within the confines of a sheet of paper or a cardboard model, and although it has a practical purpose, much of its satisfaction is derived from the play elements: the rules, the smallness, the fantasy of making space, the re-creation of childhood freedom.

Carl Jung recounted that when he was undergoing a process of self-analysis and trying, with difficulty, to understand his early memories, he decided to re-create the play activities of his childhood, or, rather, one in particular.

THE BUILDING GAME

Every day after lunch he went for a walk along the lakeshore and collected small stones, which he brought home. With these he started building miniature houses, using mud as mortar, just as he had done as a boy of ten. Although he felt foolish indulging in this childish play—he was, after all, a grown man, a family man, and a practicing psychiatrist—he continued for several weeks and produced an entire village, with cottages, a castle, and a church. "Now, really, what are you about?" he asked himself "You are building a small town, and doing it as if it were a rite!"

When I was young, I too built little buildings, although the play often took a martial turn—sandcastles and earthen fortifications, trenches and bastions, little Maginot Lines where my playmates and I would attack and counterattack with toy tanks and field artillery. But Jung's story stirred an earlier, long-forgotten memory—I must have been six or seven—of a lilliputian village built in the dusty lane behind my parents' house in Surrey. The tiny buildings were made out of stones and twigs, with cardboard roofs covered with dirt. They were agricultural in purpose, for I dimly remember little lead horses and cows, and a herd of sheep contained by pebble walls. I spent many hours playing in that lane, a solitary Gulliver expanding his little pastoral universe.

(3)

••

MAKING SPACE

I played with construction toys, but this was not the reason that I decided to study architecture. Like many middle-class immigrant children I felt obliged to enter university; it remained to choose a subject to study. The product of what used to be called a classical education, I was proficient in Latin and woefully inadequate in the natural sciences; neither physics nor chemistry interested me. I was too shy to consider law, and too queasy for medicine. I really wanted to study literature or history—as a boy I had read through a whole library shelf of G. A. Henty—but these seemed insubstantial and frivolous pursuits for the son of an engineer. Engineering, however, attracted me not at all. I needed a compromise, and architecture—a seeming blend of technology and art—offered itself. Besides, I had an uncle who was an architect, which gave me a sense of confidence; I had no relatives who were historians, let alone writers.

I knew very little about architecture as a profession—my uncle lived in Paris and I saw him only occasionally—and what I learned, I learned first from books. Or, rather, from one particular book: Frank Lloyd Wright's *A Testament*. It was hard for an impressionable youngster not to be beguiled by this individualistic romantic who wrapped the art of building in high-flown, mysterious prose. In short order I was hooked.

Part of Wright's appeal was his outrageousness. Whenever anyone asked him how he was able to produce his designs so rapidly, he would answer: "I simply shake them out of my sleeve." This was said only half-jokingly—Wright never let his listeners, or readers, forget that they were in the presence of a Great Man. But like many of his boastful statements, it was not wholly untrue. There is a record of how he designed what many consider to be his masterpiece—the house he built for Edgar J. Kaufmann on Bear Run in Pennsylvania. Kaufmann had engaged Wright several months earlier and, having received no news from the architect, he telephoned to ask if he could visit the office to review the progress made on his house. Wright agreed. With his assistants watching, he "sat down at the table set with the plot plan, and started to draw. First-floor plan. Second floor. Section, elevation. Side sketches of details, talking *sotto voce* all the while. The design just poured out of him. 'Liliane and E.J. will have tea on the balcony . . . they'll cross the bridge to walk into the woods . . .' Pencils being used up as fast as we could sharpen them when broken— H's, HB's, colored Castell's, again and again being worn down and broken. Erasures, over-drawing, modifying. Flipping sheets back and forth. Then, the bold title across the bottom: 'Fallingwater.' " According to Edgar Tafel, who witnessed this scene, Wright had visited the site once and had a topographic plan to work with, but he had not previously prepared any drawings. The whole process took about two hours.

The making of an architectural masterpiece—or indeed

any masterwork—is a mystery. But the manner in which ordinary buildings are designed is susceptible to explanation; and though we cannot plumb the wellspring of Wright's lightning inspiration, we can note that there was nevertheless a method in the execution. As architects have always done, Wright worked with pencil and paper. He did not draw painterly sketches, however, but followed the rules of the building game; and the three slices produced three specific types of representation: floor plans, cross sections, and façades or elevations. A fourth category of drawing, the perspective view, was also used by Wright to great benefit—his beautiful colored sketches are much prized by collectors today. But accurate perspectives have to be geometrically constructed and take a longer time to prepare; they are used by most architects as a way of convincing clients, not as a design technique.*

There are inherent limitations to depicting three-dimensional space on two-dimensional paper. Unlike a painter, who manipulates his medium directly, an architect works with representations, not with the real thing. He imagines a cube, but he draws a square in plan, and in section. He can draw a three-dimensional cube, as seen from the outside—or from the inside—but only from a single vantage point. These drawings are at best partial representations of the movie that is running in his imagination. Space is the stuff of architecture, yet it is impossible to depict completely—or to experience—except in a completed building.

As all architects must, Wright was able to visualize space,

---

* In the case of Fallingwater, colored perspectives were prepared, but not until several days later, after the basic design was completed.

although in him this ability appears to have been more highly developed. This facility is difficult to explain. It is not, I think, a knack or an innate skill, certainly not in my own case. Unlike a musician's perfect pitch, it can be taught, or at least learned, although the extent to which it develops in different individuals is probably a function of natural talent; very few architects would be able to imagine the bewildering array of interlocking and overlapping spaces that constitute the Fallingwater house. Nevertheless, to some degree, it is a requisite skill that every designer acquires.

It was no coincidence that Wright began with the plot plan, for the presence of a specific site is a particularity of building. Buildings are immovable. We can inhabit boats and caravans—and one day, perhaps, orbiting space stations—and although all these contain space, they lack the specificity of fixed *place* that distinguishes buildings. That is why buildings that have been reerected in museums—even when they are exhibited out of doors—look forlorn. We can admire them as objects, but we cannot ignore that a vital ingredient is missing. They are like dried flowers in a glass case, uprooted and lifeless.

Site implies singular topography but also other considerations. A building is seen as part of a setting, but it is also a place from which that setting itself is observed. The standardized ship's porthole or airplane window frames an ever-changing and finally monotonous scene; the view that is glimpsed by a well-placed window is unique and, together with the window itself, becomes a distinctive part of the experience of the room. An automobile is an object in the landscape; a building becomes a part of it, hence a landmark. Buildings, like cars, have doors; but to enter a house is to arrive at a special place, and the architect orchestrates this sense of arrival long before the house is reached, whether it is along a grand allée or, as at Fallingwater, by a curved and secretive forest track.

Buildings are immovable, but the site changes, according to both the season and the time of day. A recreational vehicle in the rain is just a wet metal box; a screened porch with wide, sheltering eaves is a place to *experience* the rain. A building is a part of the landscape, but in a winter storm it also stands protectively against the natural elements. Perhaps the most influential aspect of the site is the sun, whose movement is reflected not only in the location and disposition of different rooms but also in the design of the façades. The Fallingwater house, despite its sculptural and abstract appearance, has the glass areas carefully placed on the south side and the solid stone walls on the north.

A dramatic building site, such as Bear Run, influences the architect. Fallingwater is built on a huge boulder and straddles a stream—a stair leads down dramatically to a landing that is suspended inches above the water. But Fallingwater, like all buildings, is first of all a setting for human activity—walking, sitting, having tea. These activities are both a stimulus and a constraint. The type of space through which one passes quickly suggests different possibilities than the type in which one reposes for long periods. And human uses impose limitations. If the terrace for having tea is at a different level from the living room, the architect must provide a stair, and the risers and treads of stairs impose their own geometrical constraints. And although the terrace may appear to be "floating," it must be structurally supported with columns and beams, which also must follow enduring laws of gravity, engineering, and the strength of materials.

This combination of function and fancy makes architectural design unique, or almost so. The late historian Peter Collins once blithely proposed that building design could be better understood by means of what he called the Gastronomic Analogy. With tongue only partly in cheek, he went on to make a convincing case. Both gastronomy and architecture found their beginning in the fulfillment of a necessary human need—eating and shelter, respectively. Both were characterized by an unusual combination of science and artistry; they merged actual materials with intellectual conceits and depended on logical rules as well as imagination. Both dealt with questions of good taste instead of fashion, and both depended on—and served—patrons. Like gastronomy, architecture was intended to give pleasure, and since it was also a social art, it relied on the active participation of its public. The art of building emerges from the art of living, just as the art of cookery can be said to be the product of the art of eating.

Gastronomy—the word and the science—was a Parisian invention; and its appearance, around 1800, heralded a general appreciation of fine cooking, due largely to the earlier establishment and proliferation of restaurants. Culinary treatises such as the *Almanach des Gourmands,* or Brillat-Savarin's *Physiology of Taste,* were indispensable tools in the propagation of gastronomical knowledge. These were not mere cookery books such as had existed before but were an effort to deal rationally and methodically with food preparation. Here too the Gastronomic Analogy contains a curious parallel, for the development of architecture has similarly been influenced by books that combined philosophical speculation with rules—that is, with recipes.

The first, or at least the oldest known, example of an architectural treatise is that of a Greek-trained Roman architect named Marcus Vitruvius Pollio. Its exact date of writing is obscure—it was probably written during the reign of the emperor Augustus—and not much is known about the author, since no other record of him exists. Even the title is in dispute; it is often referred to simply as *On Architecture*. It is unlikely that Vitruvius was the only Roman architect to have written such a text, but his fame was assured by Boorstin's Law, for this was the only architectural treatise to survive that great winnowing period of ancient knowledge, the Dark Ages. It was only thanks to the copyists of medieval monasteries that a tenth-century copy of Vitruvius found its way to the library of Saint Gall, where it surfaced in 1415, just in time for the Italian—that is to say, European—Renaissance.

The impact of Vitruvius's book on Quattrocento architects was like the discovery of Piltdown Man, except that the Roman text was no hoax. Here, at the very time that the artistic and architectural accomplishments of antiquity were beginning to be held up as the only models worthy of emulation, was the missing link: an authentic voice from the past—and a necessary voice, for without this explanatory text the ruins of ancient Rome, by now decaying and already fragmentary, would have had little meaning. Moreover, Vitruvius presented his subject in an organized, rational way. This in itself was novel and contrasted with earlier works such as the construction manual of the French master mason Villard de Honnecourt, whose thirteenth-century text was an idiosyncratic, Ripley's-Believe-It-or-Not mixture of fragments of building plans, hints on carpentry and geometry, proposals for automatons, even recipes for patent medicines.

The introduction to *On Architecture* described the treatise that was to follow as a "complete system of architecture." This was an ambitious claim but one on which the author delivered. He dealt with principles of planning and design, with public and private buildings, with their visual qualities, and with such practical aspects as ventilation and plumbing. He recommended techniques for laying out building sites, for applying stucco, and for mixing paints. He explained the origins of the classical orders and the correct way to proportion and use them. Since Roman architects were also expected to be skilled in mechanics, there were chapters on machinery, bridges, and siege engines.

There was one thing about Vitruvius, however, that a sophisticated Renaissance *uomo letterato* could not fail to notice: his style and method of expression were, to put it kindly, pedestrian, and many of his terms obscure. An unkind contemporary critic said of Vitruvius, "He wrote in such a manner, that to the Latins he seems to write Greek, and to the Greeks, Latin: but indeed it is plain from the book itself, that he wrote neither Greek nor Latin, and he might almost as well have never written at all, at least with regard to us, since we cannot understand him." The critic was Leon Battista Alberti, a Florentine patrician, and he decided to remedy the situation by writing a treatise of his own—or, as some historians have suggested, by rewriting the ancient text. Following the example of *On Architecture,* Alberti organized his book (which he called *Of Built Things*) into ten sections, which similarly dealt with designing, building materials, ornament, construction methods, and different building types.

When Alberti began *Of Built Things,* in the middle of the fifteenth century, he was more than forty years old and already well known, although not yet as an architect—that pursuit lay ahead of him. He had studied canon law and was employed in the papal civil service, but his responsibilities left him plenty of time to devote himself to the study of art, science, and philosophy, and to writing. His most famous dissertation discussed the subject of the family, but he also produced celebrated works on mathematics, painting, and sculpture. He was known as an exceptional horseman (he wrote a book about that too), a witty playwright, an outstanding organist and composer, and a brilliant conversationalist. A model Renaissance man, he churned out pamphlets on a curious array of subjects: love, agronomy, grammar, public speaking, law, dogs, and secret codes. Only gastronomy eluded him.

Alberti presented a draft manuscript of his work to his employer, Pope Nicholas V, in 1452; but even before it appeared in printed form, more than thirty years later, *Of Built Things* was widely circulated and admired. Its fame lasted. "Anyone who wishes to follow the architectural profession should read Vitruvius. But let him read Leon Battista's book too, for he will find it very useful and beautiful," the sculptor Benvenuto Cellini advised in 1565. The French architect Philibert de L'Orme, who wrote his own primer, recommended Alberti to his students; Palladio too ranked Alberti's writing high. This praise reflected the almost universal respect accorded an acclaimed genius but not necessarily the usefulness of his book to the practitioner.

Alberti's preface suggested that his was more a book *about* architecture than *for* architects; and despite the wealth of technical minutiae that this book contained (the best time of year to make bricks, how to fire lime, how to make scale models, or how often to introduce landings in staircases), it is unlikely that *Of Built Things* found much use as a reference book. Most builders of the day would have been well acquainted with Alberti's recommendations, which in any case were too summary to be of practical use. This was to be expected. When Alberti wrote *Of Built Things,* he was a learned scholar but without any experience in the craft of building; and even later, when he was engaged to advise on the design of buildings, he did so only in the preliminary stages—the work was always carried out and completed by others. For despite his wealth of achievements and talent, the single word that best describes Alberti is not "writer" or "architect" but "moralist," and *Of Built Things* was meant as a scholarly discourse on the ideals governing the art of building, not as a collection of pragmatic recommendations for practice.

There was another reason that Alberti's treatise was of limited use to practitioners: it had no pictures. Here the Renaissance author broke with Vitruvius, whose text suggested that there were accompanying illustrations, although these had not survived. Alberti preferred the written word alone, perhaps because his interest was that of a theoretician, or perhaps for reasons of convenience. The German printing press was not introduced to Italy until 1465; and when *Of Built Things* was written, books existed only in manuscript form and had to be duplicated by hand copying. When drawings were included, as was sometimes the case, they depended on the talent of the copyist and were usually rough sketches. A century later, illustrations were added to *Of Built Things* (which became known as *Ten Books on Architecture*), but Alberti's original text contained none. And without drawings, a discussion of building plans, façade proportions, or ornament was dry and left all—or nothing—to the reader's imagination.

When the first illustrated technical manual—on the subject of military machines—appeared in Italy in 1472 (the year of Alberti's death), the advantage of having woodcuts accompanying text must have been striking. Soon after, in 1480, Leonardo da Vinci conceived a book on architecture which, unlike Alberti's, was to consist exclusively of drawings—unfortunately it was never published. Nevertheless, the surviving sketches are the first attempt to describe a wide variety of buildings with recognizably architectural drawings: plans, cross sections, elevations, and isometric views.

The best-known author of a designer's manual was another Italian, and neither a dilettante nor a painter but a seasoned practitioner—or, as Peter Collins would have it, a *grand chef*. Unlike the aristocratic Alberti, Andrea Palladio was of humble origin, and trained as a stone carver. He acquired his knowledge of antiquity, and his Latin-sounding name—more distinguished than Pietro della Gondola—when he was already in his thirties.* He may have lacked a noble name and a formal education, but he had qualities more important: an inquisitive mind, a good eye, and a great talent.

Palladio's *The Four Books of Architecture* appeared in 1570 and eventually became the most influential guide of its kind. It is not hard to understand why. It combined

---

* There are more recent examples of architects who have modified their names. Simple Herr Mies became the aristocratic Mies van der Rohe; the bourgeois Charles-Edouard Jeanneret made himself into Le Corbusier; Frank Goldberg, the son of an indigent shopkeeper, became Frank Gehry. Another Frank had his middle name—Lincoln—changed by a possessive mother who substituted her maiden name and produced the mellifluous appellation Frank Lloyd Wright.

Alberti's scholarship—Palladio had taken the trouble to visit and study the classical monuments of Rome—with the accumulated wisdom of a sixty-two-year-old builder of several dozen buildings. It was also profusely illustrated; as was now the fashion, Palladio accompanied his text with carefully dimensioned drawings. In addition to his renditions of ancient buildings, he included many of his own domestic designs, and it was the latter that were to influence later generations of architects.

Palladio's country houses followed a systematic layout which consisted of an entrance loggia and a central hall on the main axis, large rooms on the sides, and, between them, smaller anterooms and spaces for staircases. The dimensions that the architect included in his plans were of paramount importance, for he considered harmonic proportions the key to architectural beauty. The rooms were laid out according to strict rules of symmetry, but these were manipulated to accommodate different functional demands and different building sites. This is evident in one of Palladio's most striking designs, the Villa Capra—or, as it is more commonly called, the Villa Rotonda. In this house the hall was in the center, flanked by four large rooms in the corners, with four smaller anterooms between them. This was the architect's standard solution for a country house, but the site was unusual and required an unusual solution. "As [the house] enjoys from every part most beautiful views, some of which are limited, some more extended, and others that terminate with the horizon," the architect wrote, "there are loggias made in all the four fronts." This resulted in a cruciform plan, with a circular central hall— hence the name Rotonda—surmounted by a dome. Since one of the loggias, on the north façade, functioned as the main entrance, the plan was ingeniously contrived so as to have a major and a minor axis: the large rooms were rectangular and faced north and south, perhaps intended for summer (north) and winter (south) use; the passages from the loggias to the hall on the entrance axis were slightly wider than the others.

Resurrected by Inigo Jones, *The Four Books of Architecture* was translated into English at the beginning of the eighteenth century and formed the basis of the durable Georgian neoclassic style. In America, Thomas Jefferson was a great admirer of Palladio. He referred his friend General Cocke, who was building a house near Monticello, to Palladio's book, which he called "the Bible." "You should get it and stick close to it," Jefferson advised. That is what he himself had done when, not yet President, he had based his anonymous—and unsuccessful (he took second place)—entry to an architectural competition for the President's Mansion on the Villa Rotonda.

The usefulness of *The Four Books of Architecture* for gentlemen-builders like Jefferson was not only that it provided a large variety of floor plans that could be copied and modified to suit different building programs. The first section contained, like Alberti's book, a detailed description of the building blocks of classical architecture: the five orders. In the subsequent sections, the buildings—Palladio's own designs as well as famous monuments of Roman antiquity—were represented as assemblies of these elements, of columns, pilasters, arcades, pediments, and porticoes. At the risk of trivializing a creative genius, one could say that this was architecture explained as cooking. There was a variety of building elements (the ingredients), dimensional rules for their correct proportion and size (the quantities), and harmonious ways in which they could be combined (the cooking instructions). With Palladio in hand, any practitioner could now get it right.

ᵻ᷿᷾   ᵻ᷿᷾   ᵻ᷿᷾

These early treatises established a tradition of writing architectural primers. Such books have generally followed one of three models. First there have been practical primers such as the ornamental pattern books of the Low Countries, which assisted architects and builders in producing the fanciful strapwork gables that can still be seen on early-seventeenth-century Amsterdam houses. The Victorian catalogs of architectural spare parts that could be assembled into complete buildings by unlettered small-town carpenters also fall into this category.

Second, there have been books by practitioners who proposed a personal approach and illustrated it largely with their own projects or buildings. Few modern architects have had the wide-ranging interest of Palladio, however; and such books are usually little more than promotional *catalogues raisonnés,* collections of glamorous architectural photographs with a brief descriptive text. There have been exceptions. Le Corbusier, a painter, sculptor, architect, and town planner, who was often referred to as a Renaissance man, was also a skillful pamphleteer. In 1923, he published a historic manifesto, *Towards a New Architecture,* whose call for a stripped-down architecture was illustrated with photographs of airplanes, steamships, and automobiles. Like Palladio, Le Corbusier was also intrigued by the alchemical problem of proportioning—the secret of beauty residing in the relative sizes of various building elements. His chief contribution to the practice of design was contained in another book, *The Modulor,* which described a complicated system of dimensioning based on the Greek golden section and on the measurement of a six-foot person in various positions. The Modulor system had a limited success among his most devoted followers, but the long lists of numbers hardly explained their creator's inventive designs, which often ignored his own rules.

Wright, another rule breaker, also designed his buildings to fit the "normal" human body, whose height he characteristically based on himself. He wrote: "It has been said that were I three inches taller than 5' - 8½" all my houses would have been quite different in proportion. Probably." That was vintage Wright, cocky and ready to cloak his work in ambiguity or humor. He wrote many books, always illustrated with his own buildings, and always marred by a self-promoting prose style as impenetrable as his own outlandish public persona.* Only his last work, *The Natural House,* published in 1954 when Wright was eighty-five, broke with this pattern. In it he gathered together several essays on home design and, in a forthright, conversational style, offered advice about foundations, painting, attics and air-conditioning (he disliked both), roof shapes, and building costs. This short book, which prospective homebuilders can still read to their advantage, was as close as Wright came to writing a how-to-do-it manual.

If Le Corbusier and Wright were too interested in innovation to formulate rules and stick to them, the same could not be said of the third great architect of the twentieth century, Mies van der Rohe. His long career was marked

---

* His private letters, especially those communicating instructions to his assistants, are models of succinctness and clarity.

by an architectural rigor and a single-mindedness of purpose rarely equaled in the profession: the one hundred and twenty buildings and projects that he produced during the last thirty years of his life are so remarkably consistent that they could be described as variations on a single theme—a three-dimensional fugue in steel and glass. This most rational of designers, who was also a teacher, could have been expected to produce a rule book—he so obviously worked according to a system—but he did not. It may have been his taciturn and reclusive nature. Or was the universality that he claimed for his buildings more personal than he cared to admit and expose? In any case, like a possessive cook, he held back the key ingredient of his recipe.

The third tradition of writing was that of the theoretician. Recently, architectural theory has become an academic discipline, one that is dominated by architectural historians, whose professional bias is the classification and identification of prototypes and who have been discovering new architectural movements as quickly as the designers can get them off their drawing boards. This is history written on the run, and often by academics who are undeterred by their lack of knowledge or experience of how buildings are actually designed and built. Out of the hothouse atmosphere of the university seminar room has come a proliferation of isms: rationalism, historicism, postmodernism, late postmodernism, neotraditionalism, and, recently, deconstructivism.

Is there no contemporary Alberti, then, to enlighten and counsel the practicing architect? The most recent attempt to compile an architectural *guide culinaire* has been undertaken by the American architect Christopher Alexander. Following the example of his Renaissance predecessors, he has done this with a series of books, now numbering six, that have appeared over a decade. Taken together, these amount to a manifesto—Alexander has built little—but one that outlines means, as well as goals.

It is Alexander's controversial thesis that all great traditional buildings, despite their evident cultural and technological differences, have shared certain objective attributes, which have been combined and recombined throughout history. With a group of researchers and students at the University of California, he spent eight years compiling a list of 253 discrete environmental qualities—or patterns, as he called them. Each pattern described a relationship between space and human activity and was based on an observation of how people used buildings. For example: "A building in which ceiling heights are all the same is virtually incapable of making people comfortable." Or: "Balconies and porches which are less than six feet deep are hardly ever used." Or: "Everybody loves window seats, bay windows, and big windows with low sills and comfortable chairs drawn up to them." Alexander called his lexicon a "pattern language," and his purpose was to provide the designer with a choice of patterns with which buildings could be devised, much as sentences are created by combining words. Although the resemblance between architecture and language had been pointed out a long time before—in the 1750s, by the French architect and educator Jacques-François Blondel—no one had ever followed the linguistic analogy to this extreme conclusion.

A Pattern Language appeared in 1977, in the form of a fat little book—over one thousand pages—printed on fine, thin paper, like a dictionary—or, some said, like a missal. Alexander is a moralist, and his rationalization of the design process was intended as a sweeping critique of contemporary design. He resembles Alberti in other ways—he was educated first as a mathematician, and he too arrived at his ideas through reflection, not practice. This did nothing to mitigate his self-confidence, however, or his scornful criticism of what he considered misguided current practice. That, as well as the ambitious scope of what struck many as a preposterous project (the patterns described not only buildings but also neighborhoods and entire towns), has, at least for the moment, limited its influence on the profession.

The more successful descendants of the Renaissance treatise writers, or at least their distant cousins, were neither masters nor theoreticians. In 1936, the German Ernst Neufert published *Bauentwurfslehre,* or "rules for building design." This was a comprehensive pattern book of building types, in the manner of Vitruvius and Alberti but arranged as prototypical planning information, not as complete buildings to be copied. Neufert's aim was to "reduce, schematize, abstract the elements of design basics so as to make simple imitation difficult and to oblige the user to create form and content out of data." He accomplished this with graphics, accompanied by a minimum of text. The idea of standardization and of "types" reflected the author's background—he had been both a student and a teacher at Walter Gropius's Bauhaus. But this was intended as a practical manual, not as a polemical text—which explains why it has remained popular, and in print in several editions in all the major European languages.

The aim of Neufert's primer, or of Charles Ramsey and Harold Sleeper's *Architectural Graphic Standards,* its American equivalent, was to illustrate proven and current practice and to make sure that the information it contained would not soon be dated. The fifth edition of the latter remained unaltered for fourteen years; my own twenty-year-old copy is still useful. This is not because architectural ideas have not changed but because the authors of *Graphic Standards* were highly selective in the information that they included. In the foreword to the first edition they advised the reader: "To translate the facts more quickly for those accustomed to making and using drawings, we chose the graphic form of presentation, purposely devoid of all design in the decorative sense." I think that Alberti, who would probably have approved of the idea of a standard reference text, would have been puzzled by this statement. In *Of Built Things* he allotted equal space to necessity *and* beauty, and the idea that one could discuss architecture without reference to design or decoration would have struck him as very odd indeed.

It was odd but understandable, or at least editorially prudent, for there is no longer any consensus about what constitutes either beauty or good taste in building. Already in 1932, when Ramsey and Sleeper published their book, a rupture had occurred between "the facts" and "design in the decorative sense"; today, architectural design has become a creature of fashion. The Gastronomic Analogy, which had been proposed more than twenty-five years ago, bears this out as well. Peter Collins, who had once worked for the French architect Auguste Perret and was an avowed classicist, deplored the taste for novelty that characterized much modern building. Modern architecture, like fast food, had usurped the old bourgeois recipes. But according to Collins, the romantic and personal nature of these fashions opened the door only to improvisation, not to order. Without rules, he maintained, proper architecture could not be created. He suggested that in architecture, as in haute cuisine, true invention was extremely rare—an Escoffier or a Mies van der Rohe comes along once in several generations. According to Collins, the aim of the average practitioner—architect or cook—should be to master the skill, not to create new dishes. Getting it right should be enough.

🙾   🙾   🙾

What did "getting it right" mean in practice? To the classically trained architect it meant, first of all, pleasing the client or, in a broader sense, the user of the building (not always the same person). This unassuming, and to most persons obvious, requirement needs emphasizing in a period when architectural design has become a self-expressive pastime. The great chef Carême said, "In matters of cookery there are not a number of principles, there is only one and that is to satisfy the person you are serving." If I were to quote his advice to my students, they would find it a hopelessly old-fashioned and intolerable imposition. On the other hand the idea that the architect should design to please himself, or his muse, would have puzzled Vitruvius, who relied on patronage for his daily bread and unabashedly dedicated *On Architecture* to the emperor Augustus.

One of Vitruvius's chief promoters in the English-speaking world was Sir Henry Wotton, an English diplomat who had spent almost twenty years in Venice and who in 1624 published *The Elements of Architecture*. Wotton, who is best remembered as an angler and as the friend and biographer of Izaak Walton, was not an architect, or even a dilettante, and in his short monograph he made no claim to originality. Instead, he summarized the views of the most notable Italian treatise writers—Giorgio Vasari, Palladio,

64

Alberti, and, of course, Vitruvius. The latter had mentioned *utilitas, firmitas,* and *venustas* as the three chief concerns of the architect. Wotton pushed this statement to the fore, literally, and began his book with the following statement: "In Architecture as in all other Operative Arts, the end must direct the Operation. The end is to build well. Well building hath three conditions. Commoditie, Firmenes, and Delight."

Commodity dictated planning useful, comfortable, and agreeable spaces. As Alberti put it: "It is the business of architecture, and indeed its highest praise, to judge rightly what is fit and decent: for though building is a matter of necessity, yet convenient building is both of necessity and utility too." Firmness required that the building stand up and resist the elements over a long period of time. It also demanded that this be accomplished without waste, using an economy of structure and material. This concern was not only for the client's pocketbook but also for the avoidance of unseemly extravagance and waste. Finally, delight: this meant beauty, obviously, but it also implied both fitting in and propriety, giving pleasure to the mind as well as to the eye.

The classic ideal was one of balance, and it was not enough for a building to incorporate only one of the three; it was not enough for it to be only useful or only structurally efficient or even only handsome. "That work therefore cannot be called perfect which should be useful and not durable, or durable and not useful, or having both these should be without beauty," warned Palladio. That was what distinguished architecture from a hurriedly built shelter, or from engineering, or from a theater setting—architecture had to consider all three.

Commodity, firmness, and delight had to be combined, and the art of architecture consisted in doing this in such a way that the three became indistinguishable—that is, the various elements of the building had to incorporate all three *at the same time*. The columns that composed a classical Greek temple such as the Parthenon, for example, not only supported the roof, they formed a sheltered porch—a place for Athenians to stroll out of the blazing sun. But they were visual elements as well: the shadows created by the vertical fluting that was carved into them emphasized their height and created a beautiful visual texture. Finally, the peristyle of freestanding columns produced a striking parallactic effect on the observer walking beside or within the colonnade.

The great chimney of the Fallingwater house likewise represented a synthesis of commodity, firmness, and delight. Not only did it enclose the flues of several fireplaces (one on each of the three levels), it also acted as a structural support for two cantilevered roofs and a terrace. Most important, its large mass visually anchored the pinwheeling composition of cantilevered balconies. It was also an opportunity for Wright to use a different material—rough sandstone—which contrasted with the plain concrete of the balconies. The balustrades of these balconies were required for safety, but they were also an integral part of the structure—like the upturned lip of a tray, they reinforced the concrete shelves. Finally, their solid horizontal appearance was an important visual feature of the design.

The Wottonian-Vitruvian triple yardstick underlines the unique nature of the art of building, an art of compromise which unites the beautiful with the practical, the ideal with the possible, the ephemeral with the concrete. It is this that distinguishes it from other creative endeavors. Unlike sculpture and painting, which produce objects in space, buildings *contain* space. Moreover, it is space that is intended not only to be experienced and admired but also to be inhabited. Making space is a social art; and although architecture consists of individual works, these are always parts of a larger context—of a landscape, of other buildings, of a street, and, finally, of our everyday lives.

(4)

••

FITTING IN

E VERY small-boat sailor knows the story of Joshua Slocum, the first person to single-handedly circumnavigate
the globe. It took him three years and two months. Equally
impressive—at least as far as I was concerned—was that
the *Spray,* the thirty-seven-foot sloop in which he achieved
this feat, was almost completely homemade. In *Sailing
Alone Around the World* he recounted how he rebuilt the
derelict, hundred-year-old oyster boat that had been given
to him by a sailing acquaintance. Slocum, no slacker like
me, got down to work immediately. He felled a nearby oak,
which provided the wood for a new keel; a neighboring
farmer dragged in enough wood for the rest of the frame.
He built a steam box for bending the replacement ribs to
shape, planked them with Georgia pine, and caulked the
seams with cotton and oakum. He did all this alone, working with adz and broadax, without the benefit of power
tools—it was 1892, after all.

The forty-eight-year-old Slocum did not have electricity,
but he had something better—a wealth of experience. Over
a thirty-year career he had risen from seaman to captain
and then to ship's owner. He had built steamships and

sailing ships and fitted out whalers. A man of typically Victorian grit, he had fought cholera, smallpox, and mutinous sailors. He was nothing if not resourceful. Once, shipwrecked on the coast of Brazil, he built a canoe and with his wife and son sailed it back to Washington, D.C. A life spent on the sea was buttressed by undoubted genetic advantages—Slocum was born in Nova Scotia, at a time when this was the principal maritime region in the world. And still it took this seasoned salt thirteen months to complete the *Spray;* how long would it take me?

I think I knew what Captain Joshua would have said. "To young men contemplating a voyage I would say go," he had written. To a young man contemplating building a boat he would have undoubtedly said "go" too, and added a crusty "What are you waiting for?" I preferred the advice of Howard Chapelle, the author of a handbook on wooden boat construction: "The beginner should have no feeling of haste."

Exactly so. My dream of constructing a boat had not hardened into an obsession, and I was in no rush to start what promised to be an arduous task. I was enjoying going through boatbuilding magazines and making boat models. I had a growing collection of naval architects' blueprints, and I liked reading the archaic nautical terminology: thwarts, strakes, garboards, keelsons, words of diverse pedigree, inherited from the seafaring nations of northern Europe. I had started buying woodworking tools—planes and chisels—at secondhand shops. Wooden boatbuilding is a traditional craft (Chapelle's definitive book is almost fifty years old and is still in print); indeed, that was part of its charm and part of its attraction. At the same time, I had to admit to myself that many of the traditional skills that

Chapelle, and Slocum before him, took for granted—the ability to scarf joints, to stretch canvas decking, to cast lead keels—might pose problems.

I had other excuses for not beginning the boatbuilding workshop immediately. By the time the legal paperwork for the land transaction was concluded, it was late fall; soon it would be cold and the ground would be frozen, making excavation for foundations impossible. In any case, the land purchase had severely depleted our savings, and there would be annual payments to meet; it was hardly the time to think of building. During that winter my sketchbook filled up with drawings of sheds of various shapes.

Contentedly, I played the building game. The following summer, while we camped in the meadow, I built a picnic table. It was a modest start, but I was in no hurry.

It was after a particularly pleasant day, as we were pack-

GRAND BANKS 22, DORY

ing the picnic things into the car, that I said to Shirley, "Wouldn't it be nice to be able to stay?" Once raised, the possibility—it was hardly a plan—that we might want to build a weekend home one day was difficult to ignore. It

71

was a new ingredient that I had not previously considered, and one that I would have to take into account in deciding the location and shape of the workshop. The simplest solution would have been to keep the house and the workshop separate. But I had in mind that the large, top-lit room would make a fine garage or carpentry shop; and in the Canadian climate it would be convenient if it were attached to the house. I wanted to be sure that if the two were linked it would not be an awkward connection, which meant that I had to have some idea of what the house would, or at least might, be like.

As an exercise, I sketched a long, low, spreading house attached to the workshop. The dimensions of the boat-building workshop were constrained, but those of the house were not; and soon it began to take different shapes, like variations on a theme. It bent, one wing enclosing a court. It sprouted a greenhouse. It grew a second floor. A sauna appeared. It was idle speculation more than purposeful design; but, as I said, I was in no hurry.

One weekend in July, we invited our friend Vikram Bhatt, an Indian architect, to spend the day with us in the country. After lunch, the three of us sat at the picnic table under the old apple tree, talking. I told him about my plans for the boatbuilding workshop. I was probably showing off a little and making it sound more concrete than it really was. So I was taken aback when he asked, "Why not at least put in the workshop foundation this year? If you did it yourself, it wouldn't cost you very much. In fact, I have some free time just now—we could do it together."

Well, why not? I did not have a final plan for the house; but in most of my sketches the general shape and location

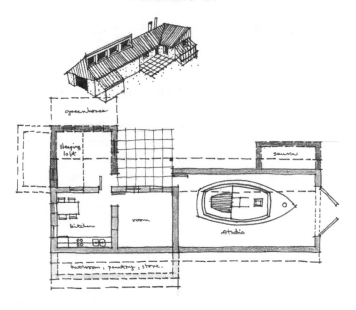

greenhouse

sleeping loft

sauna

kitchen

room

studio

bathroom, pantry, store.

A LOW, SPREADING HOUSE

of the workshop itself did not vary. It would be possible to build the workshop first; I would still have plenty of time to decide on the exact shape of the house later. Indeed, I could even build the rectangular workshop foundation before deciding exactly what would be erected on it. Although this sounds odd, it is not unusual in large, complicated buildings to begin work on the foundations before the designers have completed the upper floors. This sophisticated technique is called "fast-tracking"; in my case it was put-off-until-tomorrow-tracking. We would have to start immediately. I had to leave for the Philippines at the end of the following month, and when I returned it would be too late—both of us had other commitments. I was also concerned that Vikram's enthusiasm might wear off if I delayed. That left us three or four weeks, which was just enough time.

I remember standing on a high diving tower when I was a boy—not the low board but the one that looked like an oil derrick, with a tall ladder up one side—standing at the top, on the worn jute matting, looking down at the dark river water below. And just before I knew that I really would jump, there was a special moment. When Vikram made his generous offer, I had the same feeling, at once confusion, excitement, panic—and knowing that I would jump.

"Sure," I said. "Let's begin."

ﻭ ﻭ ﻭ

Beginnings are delicate moments, the beginning of a building no less than the beginning of a friendship or of a marriage. And how do these things begin? With a glance, a word, a phrase. Intuition, not reason, guides us, which is why the moment of beginning has often been the occasion for magic. The origin of the handshake is almost certainly magical, especially when it was used to signify the closing of an agreement—that is, the beginning of a contract. It is a wonderfully potent moment: the touching of open palms, the mutual tensing of muscles, the momentary feeling of defenselessness, and, above all, the confidence and trust demonstrated by the extended hand. There are many such practices associated with beginnings. The bride carries flowers that represent a hoped-for fruitfulness, and she is dressed in white, signifying virginity. A meal is begun with a prayer. When I was a student, my Jesuit teachers had us begin every page of schoolwork with the heading A.M.D.G.—*ad majorem dei gloriam,* "for the greater glory of God."

The city where I went to school was also inaugurated with a divine dedication. Montreal was founded more than three hundred years ago by a felicitously named Frenchman, Monsieur de Maison-Neuve—"the gentleman of the new house." He and his party of about forty persons, men and women, disembarked on the shore of the Saint Lawrence River on a bright May morning in 1642. The spot where they landed was an open meadow, bounded by the river and a stream; the land sloped up to the north to become a small mountain, which was then, as it remains today, an important landmark in the otherwise flat Saint Lawrence valley.

One might have expected that Maison-Neuve would have immediately undertaken the practical work that was needed to establish a mission in that wilderness, particularly as this was enemy territory, and the threat of the belligerent Iroquois was never far from people's minds. Instead, the entire day was spent in devotions and singing hymns. The settlers built a rustic altar in the center of the meadow, and a Jesuit priest celebrated Mass—not a hurried ceremony but a full, formal High Mass. The Sacred Host was left exposed, as if in a cathedral; this was unusual, and was done, in the words of a contemporary historian, "in order to let posterity know that He had only established this colony to receive sacrifices and honor here, that being His only aim and that of His servants, who had employed for this end alone, their wealth, their labors and their good name." As for the name of the new settlement, it was to be called Ville Marie de Montréal—the mountain had been named Mont Réal one hundred years earlier by the explorer Jacques Cartier. The town of "Mary of Mount Royal" was to be under the double protection of the Virgin and of Louis XIV, who had been crowned only three days before; Maison-Neuve's Sulpician backers were not taking any chances.*

If I were a Nabdam farmer living in northern Ghana and about to construct a building, I too would be concerned with providence. I would begin by having a chat with a soothsayer, who would tell me if my ancestors were favorably inclined to this undertaking. If the answer was yes, I would invite my friends and family to help clear a building site; this would be more than mutual help, since it would be considered unlucky if the relatives were not involved in this preparatory work. But before this, a test would have to be made to ensure that the location was a favored one. With everyone gathered in a circle looking on, a chicken would be killed and the struggling body thrown on the place where the building was to stand. The onlookers would wait anxiously for the fowl to die; would it be heads or tails? It is common knowledge among the Nabdam that if the chicken expires with its beak in the air, it signifies that the ancestors are pleased and that this is a good place to build. But if the bird dies face down, it is an extremely bad omen,

---

* What's in a name? "Ville Marie" was out of currency in less than sixty years—it was in any case unsuitable for what was already an eminently worldly city—and the town became known simply as Montréal. And Montreal it has remained, even after the French royal had been replaced by a British one: an adaptive name for an adaptive city. But Maison-Neuve was not the city's only founder; a Huron village had existed there a century before, and its name—Hochelaga—was to prove to be the most portentous of all. Montreal's—and Canada's—first prosperity was based on the trade in beaver pelts (the founder of my own university was a fur merchant); indeed, the hardworking little animal became a national symbol. Hochelaga means "at the beavers' dam."

and the builder will be obliged to find another site—or failing that, another soothsayer.

The Nabdam ceremony is contemporary, but the reliance on animals for finding "a good place" is ancient. Legend had it that Ascanius, the son of Aeneas, the hero of Virgil's epic, followed a pregnant sow and founded the town of Alba Longa on the spot where she farrowed. Alba Longa was the oldest Latin city, eventually destroyed by its rival, Rome. The site for the latter was said to have been found by Romulus after he followed a flight of vultures—apparently a more potent harbinger. These stories may have been apocryphal, but they became the basis for elaborate rituals for beginning construction that were followed during the earliest period of Roman civilization.

When a new settlement was being established, an animal—usually a sheep—was sacrificed and its liver examined. Hepatoscopy was an ancient science, dating from early Babylonia, and was widely practiced by all the civilized people of the Mediterranean, by the Hittites, the Greeks, and the Etruscans, from whom the earliest Romans inherited this practice. It identified the liver, which is filled with blood, as the seat of life, and hence with the soul. A sacrificed animal, it was believed, took on at the moment of death the soul of the god to whom it was being offered. By looking at the liver, one could, so to speak, look into the mind of the deity—that is, look into the future. The actual divination was done by inspecting the surface of the organ, particularly the size and location of the grooves that divided it into three lobes, the positions of the appendices that joined the liver to the gallbladder and the cystic and hepatic ducts, and any other surface markings. It was a complex business, but the prognostication was not improvised on the spot—

far from it. Successful interpretations were documented and recorded, and their recurrence looked for in future readings. Terra-cotta models of livers were used for teaching the future haruspex, or liver diviner, who required official certification to practice his sanguineous profession. If the signs were favorable, the site for the new town was fixed. A hole was dug into which were cast various ceremonial objects, including, for a colonial camp, earth from the settlers' home country.

Vitruvius described hepatoscopy, but by his time it was already an archaic superstition. Elsewhere, different sorts of analogous ceremonies persisted for much longer. There are several Hindu texts dealing with *silpa-sastra,* or "the science of dwelling," one of which, the *Manasara,* dates from the sixth century. The *Manasara* was a handbook for the practitioner and described the planning, design, and construction of a large variety of buildings. Everything was systematically classified; there were eight classes of villages, four classes of buildings, eight kinds of one-story buildings, five kinds of columns, and so on. The unknown author of the *Manasara* dealt with both secular and spiritual matters, and he made no distinction between the two. The chapter on foundations, for example, described the depth required for different sizes of buildings but also categorized foundations according to the four main castes. Prosaic instructions were given not only on how to determine the porosity and bearing capacity of the soil but also on exactly what plants and grains should be buried at the four corners of the building to protect its inhabitants.

The Hindu rite of beginning a building—*khat muhrat*—continues to this day. It is performed by a *shastri,* or holy man, and involves digging a hole at the corner of what will become the foundation. Into this hole, which is treated as a shrine, are placed several objects, including sandalwood paste, grains, powdered spice, and Ganges water. This ceremony is common not only for houses but for larger buildings of all types—offices, apartments, and shopping centers.

Despite the presence of Vikram, who was a Brahmin and who, in a pinch, could stand in for the *shastri,* we did not undertake any founding ritual. For one thing, there had been delays, and we were hurried by my imminent departure. For another, we were living in a pragmatic civilization—there were no spirits lurking in our future, no ancestors to placate. When Neil Armstrong landed on the moon, the culmination of a remarkable voyage and surely one of the most momentous beginnings in modern times, there was only a brief, laconic "One small step for man, one giant leap for mankind" before the astronauts got down to work with their shovels and soil samplers. We began with similar aplomb.

We were about to pay for our nonchalance. We had placed the corner stakes, lining up the long side of the building on an east-west axis. A bulldozer stripped off the grass and a layer of topsoil, which was to be replaced by crushed stone to make a pad for the concrete slab that would follow. I had engaged a local trucker to deliver the stone as soon as the excavation was complete. We waited one day, then two. I went to see him—"Definitely by the end of the week," he assured me. The promised date arrived and passed, and still no stone. I went again, primed with indignation. He was apologetic, but there was nothing he could do—a fire had broken out in his truck and he was waiting himself, for replacement parts. I commiserated, and returned empty-handed. It took another ten days before he was able to make his delivery, and whatever god we had offended underlined his displeasure further by having it rain for nine of them. We huddled dispiritedly in our tents.

Once the crushed stone pad was in place, we built a wood form around the edge of the sixteen-by-thirty-two-foot rectangle and laid a polyethylene sheet (a moisture barrier), edge insulation, and a mesh of reinforcing steel. It was not expensive; Vikram had been right—the materials cost less than eight hundred dollars. There was some wood left over, and we added a form for a little rectangle at one end—there would be a sauna after all.

The rainfall had made the field soggy, and the truck that delivered the sand and gravel had been unable to reach the building site and had been obliged to dump its load a hundred feet away. We borrowed a tractor, shoveled the material onto a trailer, and moved it to where we had installed a cement mixer. Then we loaded the sand, gravel, and cement into the mixer, fetching barrels of water from a neighbor's house. Vikram and I deposited the unwieldy concrete mixture in the form, and Shirley troweled it into the semblance of a smooth floor. It took only two days— all the time we had before my departure—two days that left the three of us exhausted, too exhausted for any sense of achievement. The day after we finished, I scraped the cement off my boots and left for Manila.

        🙠   🙠   🙠

It was travel that had brought me my first commission. Architects have traditionally gone abroad to further their education; my own grand tour, undertaken after I finished my studies, took me not to Italy but to Spain (in the footsteps of Hemingway, not of Wotton) and finally to the Balearic island of Formentera, which was then a hangout for artists, smugglers, dope dealers, and assorted sixties drifters. It was there that I met a group of vacationing Parisians. The French on holiday are a convivial people, and they be-friended me—a colonial cousin, after all—for which I was grateful, since I was traveling alone. One of them, a sculptor, had just purchased a piece of land—more accurately, rock, for it was a barren island—and finding out that I was an architect, he asked me if I would design a small house for him. My first client! Of course I agreed. Two weeks later he and his friends returned to Paris. I bought glue and cardboard, paper and pencils in the village store, set up a drawing table in an empty room of the farmhouse on which I had taken a three-month lease, and got down to work.

Sometime later I showed my drawings to Michael Shaw, an English painter with whom I had become friendly. We had spent several days together walking around the island looking for a house for him to rent, and I knew that he was interested in architecture—one of his paintings, of a white Formentera house, hangs in my sitting room. "Your house doesn't look much like the other houses on the island," he remarked after looking through my sketches. "Of course not," I answered, thinking that this was a naive reaction— I had hoped for something more insightful. "This is my own design. It's a modern house—it's not supposed to look the same." "But why not?" he asked. "Why shouldn't your house look like the others?"

I tried to respond—something about originality and personal creativity—but he remained unconvinced. Thinking back on it later, I realized that the problem was that I really didn't have a satisfactory answer. His question turned my assumptions about design topsy-turvy. I had been taught that the goal of the architect was to produce buildings that were innovative and different. In my school projects, inventiveness had been highly valued; the idea of copying existing buildings was unthinkable. In the architectural magazines and books that I pored over as a student, it was precisely the buildings that looked "different" that were praised.

Traditionally, the architect had been called upon to reinterpret forms, not to invent them, since the programmatic requirements of buildings changed slowly. Even so, occasionally a problem for which there was no precedent did present itself. In such cases, the designer could either adapt an existing building form to the new use (as Thomas Jefferson did when he modeled the new capitol of Virginia on a Roman temple) or try to invent something new. This is what Palladio did when he devised the country house in the Cinquecento Veneto, or Inigo Jones when he built the first housing terrace in seventeenth-century London, or Louis Sullivan when he established the prototype for the tall office building. The twentieth century has seen few successful examples—the drive-in restaurant and the gas station are modest but original contributions. The airport is certainly a new function, although, unlike the Victorian railway station, it has not produced a satisfying architectural resolution.

The invention of new building types is a rare occurrence. On the other hand, the idea that an architect should create new forms for *any* building is a peculiarly modern one. The pioneers of the Modern Movement—Le Corbusier, Mies van der Rohe, and Walter Gropius—were admiringly referred to as the Form Givers. Their buildings didn't fit in, they stuck out; so did the designs of their successors. No one was ever applauded for designing buildings that looked the same as all the others. But Michael's question began to nag at me. What if he was right? What if a new building needn't—indeed shouldn't—look different from its neighbors? How to proceed?

One reason that his comment struck home was that the traditional houses of Formentera—and there were no others—were beginning to grow on me. The rocky land was barren, and there were few villages; most of the houses stood alone, hardly distinguishable from the low stone walls that surrounded them. It was not that these buildings were strikingly beautiful—this was no picturesque Aegean island—but that their modest stone walls seemed right: nothing else would do in this harsh and denuded landscape. Like neighboring Ibiza, Formentera had a history of Arab occupation lasting several centuries, and many of the houses exhibited Moorish features—flat roofs, small apertures, and cool, dark interiors. Each of the three or four rooms was given a slightly different ceiling height, the main room being the tallest, which produced a pleasing variation of flat roofs on the exterior. The houses were also, as I was finding, comforting and comfortable to live in.

The more I looked, the more I became intrigued by the elusive attraction of these humble dwellings. What was their secret? I bought a tape measure and made exact drawings of the house in which I was living, the layout of the rooms, the ceiling heights, the door and window sizes. "There is nothing magic in this question of human dimensions," I wrote in my journal. "It is, rather, a matter of *fit*. Things can be put down, seen, sat on, sat in, leaned against comfortably. A door is where the person goes through; it is obviously big enough, yet not needlessly larger. It fits."

By this time I had stopped designing altogether. Instead, I walked around the island, sketching and measuring houses of friends and acquaintances and the many abandoned half-ruins that marked the most recent of the recurring droughts. I began to recognize various common features: their sturdy proportions, the way in which stone was used, the varying height of different roofs, how windows were located. In addition to the *fincas*—as the country houses were called—there were four seventeenth-century watch towers, strategically located along the coast, and four peaceful windmill towers, also disused. In the principal village of San Francisco, there was an old, fortified church. These landmarks were visible from afar in the flat landscape, the only rhetorical flourishes in the otherwise subdued domestic scene. Like the Spanish that I was slowly learning, all these architectural features represented a vocabulary. If a new house was to fit—and to fit in—it too would have to learn the language.*

Before returning to my own design problem, I assembled my drawings and notes on the traditional houses into a sort of book. At the beginning I tried to write what I had learned from this work; it was a poem—the words of a twenty-four-year-old who has just discovered that there is more to architecture than the building game.

Best to tell it from my own point of view.
Faced on all sides with unavoidable rock. Build
   on, built of.

---

* There may have been another dimension to my preoccupation with "fitting in." As a child of Polish parents in postwar Britain, as a schoolboy with an English accent, short pants, and an unpronounceable name in a small town in Canada, and as an *anglais* in French-speaking Quebec, I found that learning new languages—and new behavior—came naturally.

FITTING IN

Stand on.

Rocks that crawl up behind you. Rocks that speak
  with the moon.

In other words,

rocks.

And you are in the sun and want to get out of it
  and out of the cold wind that blows in January,
  and out of the rain, but later you will wish for
  the rain.

And it's an island you are on.

Sea and land.

Rock Sun Rain Sea Land

The Litany of the Saints

San Francisco Javier, pray for us.

But the villages are small, for sun and sea and no
  water and no electricity. And no history, or too
  much. The Moors were here, and the Romans
  who named it, and the Greeks and the
  Carthaginians and the Goths, and earliest of all
  the Phoenicians, whose graves were found on
  the island.

Their feet facing the sun. The unavoidable fact of
  the sun.

The island a rock. The rock, upon rock, a house.

Bigness and littleness.

To build a house means to rearrange the rocks.
  So simple.

And from the arrangement: shade, coolness, rest,
  a house.

Years later, I have sometimes shown the drawings of the
little Formentera house to my first-year class, as an example
of stone construction. Once, after a lecture, a student came

up to me and asked about the house, something to do with the materials or the building technique. After I answered, he said, "I didn't realize that this was one of your designs—when you showed it to us I thought it was just an ordinary farmhouse." The house differed from the local examples in several important details, but the general impression was as he had described it: the house was unquestionably plain. There was beauty in its plainness, at least in my eyes, but it was not a striking beauty that dazzled; it would take time to appreciate its unassuming charms. It was ordinary, or, rather, it was not extraordinary (which is not the same thing). In this plain and homely place, it fitted in.

ء   ء   ء

Fitting in is not generally associated with the architecture of Mies van der Rohe, who did not alter the rules of his building game whether he was playing it in frigid Montreal or sultry Havana. The Farnsworth house was his most uncompromising design; as soon as it was built, it was considered to be a landmark of twentieth-century domestic architecture. Its shape was straightforward—a flat-roofed, rectangular box, framed in steel and raised five feet from the ground. Since the whole house was supported on only eight slender columns, it had the appearance of floating above the ground. At one end there was an open porch and a large, travertine-paved, elevated platform, to be used as a terrace. What was most striking, however, were the walls—they were entirely of plate glass. The sense of floating transparency was complete since the interior lacked dividing walls and was arranged to give the impression of a single undivided space.

The house, set in a meadow beside a small river in the

Illinois countryside, its chaste geometry a perfect foil to the black sugar maples, was astonishingly beautiful. When it was designed in 1946, it had no precedents; but its evenly spaced, white-painted structure recalled a classical colonnade, and its delicate, solitary perfection was not unlike that of an eighteenth-century garden temple or a pavilion in the park of Nymphenburg or of Versailles. Like these structures, the impeccable box stood alone in the middle of a large rural property, undisturbed by the outside world. This arcadian setting was an ideal place—indeed, the only place for such an ethereal retreat.

That, in any case, is how we must imagine it, for in the intervening years the woody surroundings have lost some of their seclusion. The state park across the river has become popular—a large sign advertises canoes for rent. A new road, and a bridge only one hundred and fifty feet away, have been built, and the house is now exposed to public inspection, which so upset the original owner that she sold the house in 1968. Now the pavilion is no longer first glimpsed from a meandering footpath along the riverbank but through a car window; this unintended view is curiously prosaic—it reminded British architectural critic Martin Pawley of a mobile home.

The exquisite glass pavilion is diminished by its altered setting. And what if it had been built on a suburban lot instead of in a park? Its perfection would cease to be romantic and become merely willful; its wonderful transparency would be a liability, inhibiting the privacy of its occupants. If it were surrounded by the paraphernalia of everyday living instead of by nature, its flawlessness would collapse under the intrusive weight of a carport, a patio, a barbecue pit, a swimming pool, a cabana, a clothesline, a toolshed, and a television aerial.* Which is to say that the beauty of this house cannot be considered without reference to its context.

The Latin root of the word "context" signifies "a joining together," and the conventional modern meaning refers to the parts that immediately follow or precede a piece of writing and determine its meaning. Hence, a phrase taken "out of context" is one whose meaning has changed or become unintelligible because it is no longer a part of a larger passage. A building out of context could be one whose surroundings have changed, as happened to the Farnsworth house; but more commonly it refers to a building divorced from its surroundings, one that doesn't fit in.

The question of context is one of the most frequently overlooked considerations in building a house. People see something they like—in a photograph, on a trip, in the movies—and they say yes, that is what I want, that is how my house should be. Then they are disappointed when the result doesn't live up to their expectations—and it looked so good in *Architectural Digest!* It is thanks to magazine illustrations that we have come to perceive buildings as isolated, self-contained objects, as if they were sculptures or automobiles. It is true that a Porsche, which is both, does retain its Porscheness whether it is on a city street or in the Rocky Mountains. But buildings are always part of a context; even as self-contained a structure as the Farnsworth house relies heavily on its pastoral setting. Situate a house in different surroundings and its character changes.

---

* The house was intended as a weekend retreat for a single person with obviously spartan tastes. The present owner has added garages, an indoor pool, and accommodations for caretakers and guests. These are some distance from, and out of view of, the main house.

A house intended for a rural site, for example, will look out of place in the city—that is why farmhouses that have been overtaken by suburban sprawl look so forlorn. A home in a forest—which is to be glimpsed through the trees and discovered in fragments—would look defenseless and naked on a bare plain, just as a Spanish hacienda would be ill at ease in the rolling hills of New England. I once saw a thatched cottage on a windswept slope in Carmel, California—it didn't remind me of Devon but of Snow White and the Seven Dwarfs. Few buildings fit in everywhere. Engineered structures such as Quonset huts and geodesic domes have this dubious quality—dubious because fitting in anywhere, they seem really at ease nowhere.

The pillared portico of an antebellum mansion in South Carolina appears comfortably domestic, and surprisingly unpretentious, at least partly because of the huge plantation oaks and extravagant magnolias that surround it. Transplanted to the bare Texas plain, the same portico only succeeds in making South Fork, the home of the fictional Ewing family of television's "Dallas," look ostentatious. On the other hand, it may be the similarity of bright sun and azure sea that make the white, neo-Roman villas of Palm Beach look curiously at home.

The turrets and watch towers of Ludwig II's pseudo-medieval castle at Neuschwanstein emerge in solitary if eccentric splendor from the mists of a dense forest. The castle was meant as a retreat, like Dr. Farnsworth's glass house; however, it is anything but reticent. Ludwig was the patron of Wagner, and if architecture is frozen music, then this is *Lohengrin* in stone. But dwarfed as it is by the surrounding Bavarian Alps, its operatic pitch is not out of place. One cannot imagine this building without the dark pine forest and the enveloping mountains or not, as it is for part of the year, blanketed in snow.

The context of isolated rural buildings is the natural landscape, but most buildings have neighbors. Imagine a flat-roofed Bauhaus box in an Alpine village, or a pitched-roof structure in a Moroccan casbah, or a colonial saltbox in Formentera. Whatever the qualities of the individual buildings, however beautiful or elegant they may be, our first reaction is "They don't fit in." Such buildings are at best curiosities; at worst they simply look silly.

I have made the point that builders must learn the local language—if not, they will be outsiders, architectural tourists. The ingredients of an architectural language vary, but they can include roof shapes, window sizes, materials, colors, decorations, and proportions. The language of the boxy Balearic farmhouses is blunt and straightforward; that of suburban American houses is evocative of country villages; that of the balconied houses of old New Orleans, on the other hand, is refined, almost dissolute. It is not too fanciful to extend this metaphor and imagine that buildings in groups, sharing such a language, converse. The cottages of a Nova Scotia fishing village swap chummy smalltalk; cheek-by-jowl houses in Queens gossip affably; bourgeois brick houses along an Amsterdam canal exchange polite nods.

It is not enough to share a language; there must be propriety in the conversation: not everyone can be a star—we need supporting players as well. That is what architects mean when they talk about foreground buildings and background buildings. Ordinary homes generally fall into the second category—or at least they should. An extravagant beach house looks glamorous in the cropped photographs of the Sunday *New York Times,* but the effect of a group of such little architectural marvels on a Long Island dune is quite different. Although they have many architectural features in common—gray shingles, sloping roofs, wooden piles—the result is a noisy cacophony; they clamor for attention like traders on a stock-exchange floor.

The different shapes of buildings have developed partly as a response to different climates. A mountain chalet, for example, is intended to be snug and cozy during the long winter. The general form of the building is low to the ground and compact; the almost flat roof retains the snow to make a protective coat. A tropical house, on the other hand, is as open as possible and is surrounded by wide overhangs and sheltering verandas. A desert home is a massively built affair, with small windows and cool inner courtyards that provide relief from the killing heat. Or at least that is what it used to be. Only air-conditioning saves the California-style ranch houses of Riyadh or any of the Arab sheikdoms from being uninhabitable; nothing can save them from looking ridiculously out of place.

The early British colonialists were obliged to react to climate architecturally, since they did not have air-conditioning; and in America, Bermuda, Australia, and Kenya they developed many and varied responses to the problem of building in climates warmer than that of their temperate homeland. In tropical India they built one-story houses that they called bungalows and surrounded these with verandas.* These airy homes were well suited to the hot and humid climate of Calcutta and Bombay. It was

---

* "Bungalow" is from the Hindustani and means "from Bengal." "Veranda" is Hindi for "balcony" and was adopted from the Portuguese *varanda*. They are both reminders of the rich linguistic legacy of the Anglo-Indian period: "curry," "dinghy," "chit," "polo," "jodhpur," and also "pariah," "brahmin," "guru," "nabob," "thug."

only in the temperate climate of the hill stations that they allowed themselves to duplicate a more familiar domestic architecture; the visitor to Simla is surprised to find little half-timbered, thatched cottages surrounded by English gardens filled with English roses—a reminder of a faraway island.

Public buildings in India followed whatever style was fashionable in England. Government House in Calcutta, for example, was modeled on Keddleston, a Palladian mansion in Derbyshire; canvas awnings protected the windows, and grass mats hung between the Ionic columns of the porticoes. Eventually, the British tried to develop a specifically "Indian" form of architectural expression for public buildings. When Lutyens and Herbert Baker designed the imperial capital of New Delhi, they revived classic Moghul devices such as the protruding *chujja* cornice, the *jaali* (a pierced stone grille), and the *chattri* (an umbrella-shaped cupola). Their approach was in marked contrast to that of George Gilbert Scott, who had designed the University of Bombay. The medieval convolutions of High Victorian Gothic look distinctly odd today, surrounded by palms and banyan trees instead of ivy and oaks.

Scott's buildings ignored their tropical surroundings, but they did fit into another type of context—a cultural one. The British authorities intended these outlandish northern forms to symbolize what were, for their Indian subjects, alien institutions and alien British values. The Gothic shapes were a conscious cultural reproduction, just as Ludwig II's castle was a re-creation of the knightly fortresses of the Rhine and evoked the legendary Teutonic heroes of Wagner's operas, which he so much admired.

What would Neuschwanstein mean if it were deprived

of its cultural context? When Walt Disney built a Ludwig-esque castle in the center of his Magic Kingdom in southern California, he reduced the brooding eagle's nest to cheerful and sunny kitsch. When William Randolph Hearst built his castle, Casa Grande, in the hills above San Simeon, his aim, like Ludwig's, was to re-create the past. But the Bavarian monarch, mad as he was, was at least a king, and a German king. Hearst had not inherited a crown, only a newspaper; and the result of his fantasy, as Orson Welles demonstrated in *Citizen Kane,* was characterized by bathos and futility. Despite his architect Julia Morgan's skill and the beautiful landscaping, we remain unconvinced. What is this Italian villa doing in the California Coastal Range? The Greek and Roman statuary stare uncomprehendingly at the modern dance floor, and an ancient temple serves as a poolhouse; Sienese banners and Gothic stained glass decorate the pompously named Refectory, where movie stars dined on linen tablecloths with paper napkins. The front of the house resembles a Spanish mission; there are campaniles, church bells imported from Belgium, and statues of Saints Peter and Paul flanking the entrance. What are we to make of it? Hearst gave huge and expansive parties— that was his home's main function—and this indiscriminate assortment of architectural fragments makes sense only as a costly piece of theatrical decor, a make-believe setting for the make-believe heroes and heroines of Hollywood whom he entertained. Hearst's wife once said of Casa Grande, "The whole place is crazy." A building that ignores its context *is* crazy, because it lacks a crucial ingredient—meaning.

(5)

●●

JUST A BARN

MANILA had been hot and humid—the slum where I
had been working even more so—and it was a relief
to come back to the mild temperatures of a Canadian Indian
summer. The weekend after I returned, Shirley and I visited
the building site. Walking through the meadow, we reached
the flat concrete pad. It reminded me of an archaeological
ruin: purposeful yet mysterious, like the prehistoric stone
monuments of Carnac, in Brittany, whose function eludes
us. It could have been dropped from the sky by extra-
terrestrials. Once, flying south to New York, I identified it
from the air—it resembled a white tennis court, a perfect
rectangle in an undisturbed green field. For another nine
months it remained the only evidence that building activity
was taking place.

I had the firm intention of resuming the construction of
the workshop the following year. The building game gained
considerable impetus from this deadline, and it was also
compelled by the not unwelcome discipline of the actual
shape and dimensions of the concrete pad. The next eight
months were taken up with more drawing, done in large,
eleven-by-fourteen-inch spiral-bound sketchbooks made in

New York by the Morilla Company, whose trademark, by curious coincidence, was a three-masted schooner. I had been using these books for several years to keep a graphic journal, and in their pages I recorded the evolution of my design, month by month.

October–November

The reason that the foundation work proceeded so quickly was that at the last minute Vikram and I had reduced the dimensions of the concrete slab to a minimum, leaving only enough space for building the boat hull. If I wanted additional room for sleeping, I would have to provide this in a loft or gallery at the east end, above the small rectangle that represented the future sauna. This produced a building with a two-story section at one end, adjacent to a tall workroom, at whose western extremity were a pair of large doors through which the finished boat would eventually be withdrawn. I located another loft at this end, to provide extra space for storing boatbuilding materials. This loft extended beyond the end wall and made a sheltering overhang above the doors. The roof over the lofts ran the entire length of the building; above the workroom it became a clerestory.

My sketches showed a shingled, rustic building that could have been a Victorian boathouse, sans water, of course. It had a romantic appearance, with heavy brackets, a small porch over the door, a large bay window, and a red roof with green trim. For the moment I set aside the question of how the workshop might be connected to a future house.

A VICTORIAN BOATHOUSE

December–January

I concentrated on developing the east end in more detail.
A sleeping loft sounded simple enough, but by the time I
was finished I had added some basic amenities, including
a minuscule toilet, a shower (next to the sauna), and a
cupboard for the pump and waterheater. The utilities were
located together at one end of the building, which suggested
that a wing containing the future house could be conveni-
ently added to this side.

Although the tiny quarters were planned with the ingenu-
ity of a Pullman sleeping compartment—or a ship's cabin—
I was unable to confine them to the six-foot width of the
sauna. They expanded like yeast and pushed themselves
into the boatbuilding space. Reluctantly, I reduced the
workroom by a couple of feet. What about a place for hang-
ing clothes? And just a little extra space for a ship's ladder
(a real stair required too much room)? I lost another two

97

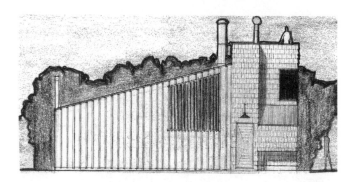

THE SECOND VERSION

feet. Anxiously, I checked my boat plans. I would have to squeeze myself around the bow and stern; but it would do—just barely.

The roof of the workroom had changed and was now a long shed, sloping down from the sleeping loft to the lower, west end. I made the ceiling of the bedroom flat, which allowed me to provide a small roof terrace—a poop deck—which was reached by the ladder, leading to a hatch. The building was beginning to resemble a coastal freighter (beached in a meadow), with the cabins piled up at the stern, and the long workroom (the hold) extending to the bows. The chimney of the woodstove (a smokestack) completed the nautical effect.

February–March

I drew the workroom. On the face of it, this was a straightforward space. Its main requirement, like that of a garage, was to have an open area with no interfering columns, and a sufficiently large entrance. These requisites were simple

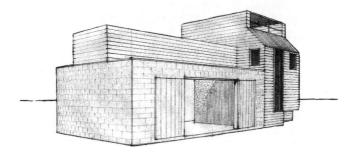

TWO LITTLE BUILDINGS

but relatively inflexible. The scale of this large room—its high ceiling, its wide doors, the greater span of the structure, and the undivided space itself—was quite different from that of the snug cubbyholes of the living quarters; I started to emphasize this difference. Since I was thinking of clerestories and skylights instead of windows, the walls were blank; and since the workroom did not need to be well insulated, its walls were made out of inexpensive concrete blocks, which contrasted with the wooden siding of the living section. When I was finished, instead of a single structure, two little buildings stood side by side in uneasy intimacy. I recognized my own ambivalence about this boatbuilding business—was I building a boatbuilding workshop or a house?

April–May

There is a moment in the design process, after one has examined various alternatives and still not produced a satisfactory solution, when nothing will do but to reconsider

99

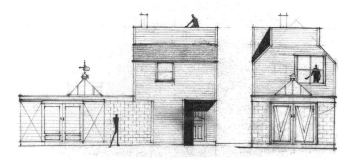

A FUNCTIONAL SOLUTION

one's initial assumptions. At this point it had become obvious that something had to be done about the competition
for space that had developed between the voracious living
quarters and the workroom. For some time I had been
concerned that my original plan to build a dory ketch was
too ambitious. There was a smaller design—a catboat—
that appealed to me and would also allow me to reduce the
length of the workroom. The living quarters advanced res-
olutely forward, lopping several more feet off the workroom
and occupying slightly more than a third of the total length
of the concrete slab.

Having resolved the question of function, I turned my
attention to the appearance of the building—no longer the
romantic Victorian boathouse of six months ago. My
sketches show an unsentimental flat-roofed building, taller
at one end and shaped a bit like a shoe. It looked . . . well,
"functional" was a kind description—like one of those buildings one sees beside a railroad track, housing switching
equipment or spare parts. Since I had located the concrete
slab in the center of a flat meadow, there were no trees—

except for the solitary apple—to obscure the building, no hillock to shelter against, no place to hide. The workshop was fully visible from the road (which was about eight hundred feet away), as one approached across the meadow, and from the surrounding farms. And what did my hard little industrial building have to do with the nearby barns and farmhouses? Very little. It was ten years ago, almost to the day, that Michael Shaw had told me, "Your house doesn't look much like the other houses on the island." I realized with dismay that much the same could be said of my present design. I had to face it: this ungainly little edifice stuck out like the proverbial sore thumb.

ᴥ   ᴥ   ᴥ

It had been easy for me, as a stranger, to observe the language of the houses of Formentera. Here, at home, I had been taking my surroundings for granted, and I would have to make an effort to understand their too-familiar language. There were two types of buildings in the place where I was building—barns and farmhouses. Both had steep, sloping roofs; flat roofs were almost nonexistent. The barns were low, straightforward structures, less imposing than those of the Pennsylvania Dutch, with few openings in their weatherbeaten wooden walls. The houses, smaller versions of the barns, were constructed of wood, stone, or brick and were distinguished by porches and galleries. They were hardly pretty, but the strong, simple shapes, half buried in drifting snow, were a comforting sight in the winter landscape. They had a Canadian reserve which valued the useful and was suspicious of the showy. They exhibited no frills, no wasted gestures. They were close-mouthed—get inside and keep warm, they said gruffly, and shut the door.

It was a question of fitting in not only with the surrounding buildings but also with the building site itself. I had oriented my foundation so that the building would be approached facing the long side of the rectangle, which would produce the sensation of a more imposing presence. This architectural "trick" is a common one; several of Palladio's country villas give the viewer the impression of great size, although the long, flanking wings of rooms and outbuildings are only one room deep, and the living quarters themselves are not large. But the present broken silhouette of my boat-building workshop—high at one end and low at the other— did not enhance this frontal effect and suggested that the building was facing in another direction. One would have had the unpleasant impression of arriving at the side door.

But making analogies with the past can be misleading. Palladio's villas, like plantation homes and English country houses, could afford to take center stage—they were big enough to carry it off. Even the Farnsworth house derived much of its poise in the landscape from its ample dimensions—the glass box measured twenty-nine by seventy-seven feet, about four times the area of my little slab. There is no way that a small building can dominate its setting; nor should it attempt to put on architectural airs—it will only appear self-important. The everyday, agricultural surroundings of my site precluded a romantic or pavilionlike structure; this was neither a park nor a wilderness. Since it couldn't hide, the workshop would have to rest in full view, not ostentatiously but plainly, the way that an isolated hay barn sits comfortably in the middle of a field.

Looking through a book on the history of barns in North America, I came across a photograph of a barn overlooking the Saint Lawrence River, on the Ile d'Orléans, near Quebec City. It was a long, low, rectangular building with a steep, gabled roof, broken only by the dormer of the hay door. What caught my eye was the uncompromising way that this prosaic building presented its broad face to the viewer. It had no cupolas, no decorations, no sheltering overhangs, no obvious "architectural" features of any kind; the bluntness recalled its frugal Breton ancestry. The whitewashed wooden walls were punctuated by several small windows and other openings, located apparently at random but presumably according to functional requirements unknown to me. There were three different doors of varying sizes, which, according to the accompanying text, provided entry for the wagon to the threshing floor, for animals to the byre, and for hay to the hayloft. A fourth, smaller door was obviously intended for humans. Something about this insistence on "fit" struck a chord—it reminded me of the Formentera houses.

I kept returning to this photograph, until I realized that what I was looking at could be my boatbuilding workshop. Of course, I planned to use the floor for lofting, not threshing, and to store a boat hull, not a hay cart; but the way in which the so-called Quebec connected barn sheltered diverse functions under one, unbroken roof appealed to me. It lent dignity and presence to this otherwise modest building. I liked its spare fenestration and its air of careful restraint. It fitted.

After almost two years and two full sketchbooks, I was going to build . . . a barn. Not even a bicycle shed—a cowshed.

*   *   *

Like many boys, I had had a stamp collection. I must have been influenced by my father, who had a homemade album of postwar Polish stamps. They were drab and crudely printed, with pictures of unsmiling politicians and unknown (to me) patriots. I preferred the British Empire, whose stamps were illustrated with camels and palm trees and the familiar royal profile of George VI, accompanied by exotic currencies—annas, pies, and piastres. By the time I was nineteen, stamp collecting had become an activity I pursued halfheartedly, with that sense of obligation which marks the imminent demise of a hobby. However, I do remember a particular Canadian five-cent stamp that was issued that year. It depicted a Victorian gent with a large white mustache and side-whiskers and a military bearing; in the background was an old-fashioned steam locomotive and a railroad bridge. The stamp, which marked the hundred and fiftieth anniversary of the man's birth, was undistinguished; what attracted my attention was the inscription "Gzowski"—one of those Polish names whose crowded consonants I had previously encountered, at least on stamps, only in my father's collection.

Sir Casimir Stanislaus Gzowski—he was knighted by Queen Victoria—was a prominent public figure in Upper Canada, as Ontario was then called. An engineer by training, he had been the provincial superintendent of public works and, as a businessman, the builder of many bridges, harbors and canals, and railroads. He laid out Yonge Street in Toronto as well as the park system around Niagara Falls; but the international bridge that he built to link Fort Erie and Buffalo, like his own mansion, no longer exists.

One structure, however, has survived. In the 1850s, a friend of Gzowski—with the Dickensian name Squire Strange—had asked him, as a favor, to undertake a modest construction project. The no-nonsense solidity of the square

granite building that still stands in the small town of Rockwood, Ontario, is a reminder of the military background
of its designer, who had held a commission in Czar Nicholas's Imperial Russian Engineers; but it is neither a casern
nor a powder magazine. Despite its carefully positioned
windows of pleasant proportions, the dressed stone at the
corners, and an elegant carved parapet at the gable ends,
this unpretentious, shedlike building is unmistakably a
barn.*

Gzowski was a man of refined temperament: his father
had been a count; he himself was a gifted linguist, a musician, an articled lawyer (in New York State), and, like
any well-educated Polish aristocrat, a skilled swordsman.
I wondered how this immigrant had designed *his* barn. At
the time, Gzowski's company was engaged in building the
Grand Trunk Railway—from Toronto westward to Sarnia,
and passing through Rockwood—and he must have been
preoccupied with the financial wheeling-and-dealing and
land acquisition that accompanied railroad work in the
nineteenth century. Did he produce a scribbled sketch on
a starched shirt cuff and pass it hurriedly to a subordinate?
Or was the barn a pleasant distraction—several evenings'
digression from his serious work?

These questions must remain unanswered, for this minor
building did not merit the attention of Sir Casimir's biog-
raphers. But the fact that a formally trained professional
should undertake to design a barn did interest me. This
surely put to rest the notion that an irreconcilable differ-

---

* This barn fitted into its surroundings as deftly as its immigrant designer—
who became the president of the Jockey Club, a colonel in the Canadian
militia, and an Anglican—adapted to his.

ence separated sheds and cathedrals. This conclusion was strengthened as I pursued the subject further and discovered that the active involvement of architects in designing farms and farm buildings went back long before Gzowski to at least the sixteenth century. The rural villas built by Palladio often included barns and outbuildings. In 1615, the Italian architect Scamozzi published a plan for a complete farm; and forty years later John Webb, a pupil of Inigo Jones, produced a rectangular compound which consisted of a farmhouse, stables, cowsheds, and barns—the first formally designed farm in England. It was not until more than a century later, however, that architect-designed barns became commonplace.

The second half of the eighteenth century was the heyday of the British "improved farm" movement, when the ideas of agricultural reformers were taken up by wealthy landowners, by aristocrats, even by mad George III, whose nickname was "Farmer George." Although many of the improvements concerned farming techniques and more efficient estate management, as well as technological aids such as steam engines and threshing machines, architects also played a prominent part in the movement, writing treatises, producing pattern books, and, of course, building buildings. Farms attracted the most illustrious Georgian architects, such as Robert Adam, John Nash, and Sir John Soane, who were pleased to provide progressive gentlemen farmers with an appropriate architectural setting.

The appearance of these buildings varied. Samuel Wyatt, an architect-engineer who specialized in farms, adopted a robust and austere neoclassical style; like Palladio, he favored plain surfaces and sparse ornament, which were well adapted to the skills of rural builders and to rural locations.

His monumental brick barn for the Earl of Leicester, which was built in 1790 in Norfolk, is difficult to date—it could be a Roman granary or a Victorian factory. The inventive talents of Robert Adam—the father of the Classical Revival—were evident in his prolific farm designs. The earliest were in the simple Tuscan style, with plans of great geometrical elegance and utility. These Georgian farms were not merely warmed-over rural versions of town buildings. Adam and other eighteenth-century architects were interested in the primitive roots of Greek architecture, and the farm seemed to be just the place to explore such ideas. This search for a rustic classicism—and lower building costs—produced not only buildings with thatched roofs and tree trunks for columns but also technical experiments with earth walls, timber construction, and tar-paper roofing.

Across the Atlantic, gentlemen farmers also concerned themselves with the appearance of their farms. Farmer George Washington built his first barn in the 1780s at Union Farm, one of five holdings into which he had divided Mount Vernon. Washington, an enthusiastic if not always successful agriculturalist, carried on a long correspondence with Arthur Young, a noted English "improver," and Young provided a plan for an up-to-date barn, which the Virginia planter duly built. The one-hundred-foot-long building consisted of a barn flanked by symmetrical cattle sheds, which were linked by carefully planned passages through which fodder was distributed. A decade later, the now-retired President undertook the construction of a second barn, this time of his own design. Polygonal in plan and built of brick, the sixteen-sided structure had two floors; a long ramp led up to the circular threshing or treading floor, around which oxen were driven. Washington was said to have been particularly proud of this barn and intended to build a similar structure on one of his other farms.

Thomas Jefferson's architectural accomplishments are well known, although no designs for barns have been recorded. In the early 1800s, however, a close friend and neighbor, General John Hartwell Cocke, did build a "Palladian barn," which, while not designed by Jefferson, is believed to have been influenced by the architect-President. The idea of dressing a barn in ancient Roman apparel, with pedimented portico and classical columns, represented a curious direction in barn design. John Soane, after a visit to Sicily, designed what he described as "a barn à la Paestum" for a Warwickshire client. The simplified brick Doric order and the pedimented roof of this elegant little structure are engaging, although the sight of a cow exiting a Greek temple must have been unsettling. In several designs for Scottish farms, Adam developed equally idiosyncratic solutions in what came to be known as the Castle Style, which was characterized by a profusion of turrets, embrasures, and crenellations. Castellated cowsheds became popular and represented a romantic tendency that was to continue into the nineteenth century.

An English book on house design, published in 1870, pointed out that barns and stables were a necessary part of any proper country estate but observed that such utilitarian buildings "mostly form a portion of the offices which are placed out of view, concealed by plantations or shrubbery, and generally at some distance from the mansion to which they appertain." The architect-author, attempting to redress this situation, went on to present a design for a building that contained a riding house, a stable, and a coach house and incorporated such advances as a circular-ribbed, cast-iron roof covered with glass, above the riding area. Nevertheless, he felt it necessary to cloak such modern materials in a veneer of gentility. The brick façade, in the Castle Style, sported a prospect tower, battlements, and other medieval features that camouflaged the sheds as effectively as "plantations or shrubbery."

Not all barns designed by architects were "dressed up." The Ames family were builders of the Union Pacific Railroad and the major patrons of the celebrated architect H. H. Richardson. In 1880, F. L. Ames asked Richardson to design an icehouse for Langwater, his estate in North Easton, Massachusetts, which was planned by Richardson's friend the landscape architect Frederick Law Olmsted. The wood building, in which ice cut from an adjacent pond was to be stored, was never built, but what is striking about Richardson's sketches is that they showed a building with a straightforward, undisguised, and unmistakably barnlike appearance; he even included an attached silo storage tower.

If some American barns were more modest in appearance, others were strikingly cathedral-like. One of the great barns of North America was built in 1892 in Shelburne, Vermont. It was designed by the New York architect R. H. Robertson for Dr. William Seward Webb, a wealthy manufacturer of railway cars, whose thousand-acre estate on the shore of Lake Champlain had also been laid out by Olmstead. The Webb barn was a wood structure, almost a thousand feet long, and included, in addition to stables and coach houses, an exercise hall and a horse-breeding barn, both lit by large dormer windows. The breeding barn was so large that it dwarfed the several grain silos that were later built inside it. This palatial complex was covered by a single sweep of roof, broken by oversized dormer windows and crowned by a graceful lantern.

Another giant barn was also paid for by railway money. It was built in 1899 by the notable Montreal architect Edward Maxwell for the Saint Andrews, New Brunswick, farming estate of the Canadian tycoon Sir William Van Horne, builder of the Canadian Pacific Railway. Maxwell, who with his brother later planned the famous Château Frontenac Hotel in Quebec City, produced a handsome timber building with a gambrel roof, which was unmistakably a barn, albeit a grand one. The complicated layout accommodated horses, cows, pigs, and other animals. Maxwell, himself a gentleman farmer, was knowledgeable about the workings of barns and designed several others during his career, though none so impressive as this one. The entrance was located in the center of the side wall, between two tall tapered silos that were capped with dovecotes shaped like cupolas and resembled medieval gate towers. In a sly piece of symbolism, the circular room at the base of the phallic silo housed Sir William's prize breeding bull.

What is striking about these late-nineteenth-century North American barns is what they demonstrate about the attitude of their designers. These architects did not wrap the buildings in architectural finery in an attempt to turn them into fit candidates for the winner's circle.* Large and refined as these buildings were, they used the vernacular of the farm and of the countryside. These were barns; they

---

* The barn that Frank Lloyd Wright built for himself at Taliesin is also in a vernacular idiom; a hexagonal barn designed and built by an assistant in Wright's absence had so displeased him that he had it demolished.

could not be mistaken for Greek temples or Scottish castles.

Practicing architects have always been less doctrinaire than art historians; as working professionals they have been obliged to undertake all sorts of commissions—cowsheds as well as cathedrals. In 1882 Richardson, by then unquestionably the leading architect of the United States and about to begin designing the All Saints Episcopal Cathedral for Albany, undertook a commission for a small barn. Obviously neither he nor Maxwell nor Sir Casimir Gzowski had felt that it was beneath him to design a barn. Nor did I.

ta   ta   ta

I had been attracted by the photograph of a Quebec connected barn. Now I had to adapt its arrangement of several functions side by side under one roof to my boatbuilding needs. I could easily imagine how the smaller rooms could serve as the living quarters. What about my workshop? The largest space in a Quebec connected barn was devoted to storing wheat or hay and was divided into three bays. The wide doors were placed in the side wall opposite the middle bay, which allowed a wagon to be pulled into the center and to be unloaded into the two side bays, which were used as granaries or haymows. At harvest time the wood floor of the central area was used for threshing.

I was no more knowledgeable about barns than the average urban architect, and I found myself intrigued by what I read about these buildings, which were so familiar and about which I knew so little. Like formal architecture, barns have undergone a long evolution. Although words such as "timeless" and "unchanging" are often used about barns, they serve only to obscure the fact that these buildings have changed over time, sometimes rapidly. These modifications were in response to innovations in materials (the availability of wooden shingles or cheap nails, for example), to improvements in building techniques, and, of course, to changes in farming practices. This suggests that the designers of common farm buildings, who were usually the farmers themselves, were no less inventive than trained architects. After all, someone had to introduce the changes that transformed the barn from one time and place to another, and which produced distinctive regional variations of the "ordinary" barn.

Just as the Gothic cathedral developed differently in England, France, and Germany, the barn has assumed different forms in different parts of the world. The exact origins of the three-bay plan, for example, are obscure, as is so much of the early history of the barn; but it is known to have existed in Europe in the seventeenth century, and examples have been documented in Quebec as early as 1662. Unconnected three-bay barns were also common in the northeastern United States, where they were introduced (somewhat later) by British immigrants and came to be known as English barns. Often a second door was provided in the opposite wall, to permit the wagon to drive straight through; and although manual threshing is a thing of the past, this arrangement continues to be used. A variation of the three-bay barn in the warmer southern states is the so-called two-crib barn, in which the central bay is an open-air breezeway.

Granaries are found in all parts of the world; but barns, for storing hay and for providing shelter for animals and a protected space for indoor threshing, are restricted to intemperate climates. It was in that respect that the New

World, especially Quebec and New England, differed from Europe—winters were longer and more severe, and the growing season shorter. With only a single harvest, barns had to be bigger than their Old World counterparts to provide space for storing more fodder and grain; and it is the size of the North American barn that is its most characteristic, and memorable, feature.

The long, connected barn of Quebec, like the three-bay English barn, was a single-story structure; but elsewhere, two-story barns were common. The farmers of mountainous Bavaria and Switzerland built barns that were dug into the side of a hill, so that they could be entered directly from grade at different levels—the ground floor being accessible from the front, and the upper level from the opposite side, higher up the slope. The lower floor, which was half-buried in the earth and easier to heat, was for the animals; the colder upper floor, for storing wheat or hay. In cases where the slope of the hill was not steep enough, earth would be banked against the rear wall to form an access ramp. The banked barn was first introduced to North America by German immigrants to Pennsylvania, where it is known as a Sweitzer barn. It also became common in Ontario—the building that Gzowski designed for Squire Strange was a banked barn.

There was a problem, however, with adapting these types of barns to boatbuilding. My site was perfectly flat, so a banked barn was out of the question. Nor was the three-bay barn suited to my needs: I didn't require storage bays; but, more important, the doors were in the wrong place—I would have to provide extra space to be able to maneuver the boat through the side doors. After examining various alternatives, I soon came to the conclusion that the most convenient position for the doors would be in the end wall, so that the finished boat could be pulled straight out of the workshop.

I was surprised to learn that a barn that suited my requirements—that was entered from the end, not from the side—not only existed but was probably the oldest type in history. The ancient Saxon cruck barn of England, Holland, and Germany consisted of a series of timber bents (called blades), rising from the ground to form inverted V's, and fastened together at the ridge and supporting longitudinal roof timbers. To make the building wider, the walls were built independently of the blades. Since these walls were too low to provide an entrance for the tall hay wagons, or wains, the natural location for the doors was in the end wall. Like the three-bay barn, the cruck barn was divided into three parts, but longitudinally, not transversely, the side spaces being used for hay storage and for animal stalls.

To provide more headroom in the barn, curved timbers were sometimes used for the blades, producing a pointed arch, which some historians have suggested was the forerunner of the masonry Gothic arch. It is hard to avoid the conclusion that the cathedral builders were influenced by barns. The oldest surviving church in Britain is Saint Peter-on-the-Wall in Essex, built around A.D. 660. It is a distinctly barnlike, rectangular, gable-roofed structure, of reused Roman material, with the door, like that of a cruck barn, in the end wall. The structure of the original timber roof, long gone, would have been exposed, as all church roofs were until the Norman Conquest; and like the interior of a cruck barn, it would have resembled an overturned ship.*

---

* The English word "nave" derives from the Italian *nave,* "ship," and surely refers to the interior appearance of the cruck barn.

JUST A BARN

Unlike churches, cruck barns were built out of perishable materials, and few examples have survived. Medieval monastic barns, on the other hand, were built of stone. Religious orders such as the Cistercians controlled vast agricultural estates, called "granges" after their principal building, the barn. The abbey at Chaalis, near Paris, was the center of a holding that comprised several thousand acres, divided into more than a dozen granges, each with its own barn. These were huge structures—the thirteenth-century grain barn that still stands at Vaulerent is seventy-six feet wide and two hundred and forty feet long. According to Cistercian practice, they were unadorned, and the severity adds to their beauty. The gable roofs were supported by pegged trusses instead of crucks, but the layout remained as before: a long central space flanked by aisles, and with the door at one end. No wonder that historians call this a "basilican plan."

The basilican plan remained popular in Holland longer than it did in Britain and France; and in New York State, Dutch settlers built barns with the doors at one end, which became known as Dutch barns. In New England, the basilican plan arrived later, during the nineteenth century. Before 1830, barns were traditionally of the three-bay, English type. The attraction of the ancient basilican plan was that it could be indefinitely enlarged by adding additional bays at one end. This was an important advantage for the increasingly productive farmers, whose crop yields were rising steadily; and according to architectural historian Thomas Hubka, within only thirty years the English barn layout was abandoned in favor of the basilican plan, which became so popular that many English barns were converted to the new arrangement. As in the cruck barn, the doors were always in the end wall, or more commonly at both

ends, so that a wagon could be driven straight through—
or a boat pulled straight out.

It appeared that my boatbuilding barn would be a hybrid,
a combination of the Quebec connected barn and a basilican
plan; I liked the idea that, through the latter, it would be
a distant relation to the medieval cathedral—*pace* Professor
Pevsner.

The most distinctive feature of a barn—as indeed of many
churches—is its large steep roof. The earliest barns were
covered in thatch, and the gable roof had to be steep to
throw off the rain and melting snow. But even when improved roofing materials such as shingles became available,
the steep slope remained, to provide the largest possible
attic volume under the roof. It was this concern for storage
space that produced another characteristic barn roof, the
gambrel. The gambrel, or hock, is the joint in the upper
part of a horse's leg, and it is an appropriate word to describe
the double-sloped, bent shape of this roof, under which
headroom and storage space are greatly increased.

The gambrel roof first appeared in house architecture
during the seventeenth century, when it was known as a
mansard. The term was derived from the French *mansarde,*
which meant a room under the roof, provided with dormer
windows. To make these rooms more commodious, the roof
was given a broken profile, with the lower face almost vertical and the upper face slightly sloped or flat. This attic
space was used to house servants. Whether or not the great
baroque architect François Mansart really invented this solution, mansard roofs became a standard feature of French
domestic architecture during the reign of Louis XIV. A log
house with a mansard roof was built in Montreal as early
as 1688.

What is curious is that there is no evidence, either in Quebec or anywhere else, that the gambrel roof was used on barns before the middle of the nineteenth century. There is no technical explanation for this two-hundred-year delay, so the absence of evidence may be the result of Boorstin's Law, or it may be an indication that in barns, as in formal architecture, the influence of fashion is not absent. It was undoubtedly fashion that produced a beautiful refinement of the gambrel roof that is still a characteristic of many Quebec barns—the gentle bell cast of the lower slope of the roof. Requiring considerable additional effort by the carpenter, this architectural feature has no functional imperative; it is final proof, if such is needed, that the barn builder too is concerned with aesthetic appeal.

Determining the shape of the roof is the most important decision that the designer of a building must make. The roof protects the building and its inhabitants from sun, rain, and snow and provides the sense of shelter that Frank Lloyd Wright felt was an essential ingredient of any building. Think of a Chinese pagoda, a Bernese farmhouse, or a Tahitian longhouse, and you think first of the roof. In different parts of the world I have seen buildings without walls, without doors and windows, even without finished floors, but never without a roof. But it is more than a functional architectural feature. Like the hearth or the front door, it has established deep cultural roots of which the language itself is evidence. "Roof" has come to mean the home itself, as when we say "a roof over one's head" or "together under one roof." That is why the cubist designs of the architects of the twenties and thirties never gained public favor—a building without a discernible roof looks naked, unfinished, and uninviting.

TOGETHER UNDER ONE ROOF

I chose a gable roof for my barn. A gable roof would be easier to construct than the more complicated gambrel; in any case, storage and headroom were not my main concern. And there was another reason. Overlooking my building site, several hundred feet away, was a collection of barns belonging to my neighbor Wilmer Sample. Cézanne would have appreciated the large cubic volumes and bulky geometry. Their gray, weathered mass—all gable-roofed—dominated the landscape; and if my building was to fit in, it could only be as a little offspring of these heroic leviathans.

(6)

CHRYSALIS

THERE is something so direct and unaffected about an architectural drawing that it is easy to forget that although it appears to be an objective representation of reality, it may be as much an illusion as a painting by Magritte. The most commonly reproduced drawing of the Fallingwater house shows the complex interpenetrations of the overlapping, pinwheeling terraces as they are seen from above. But, unless one were to pass over the house in a balloon, this aerial view remains an aspect of the design that is inaccessible to the normal visitor—it is an abstraction. Even more hypothetical was an architect's drawing that was published when plans for the new headquarters of AT&T in New York were unveiled; the handsome drawing depicted a tall office building with a prominent Chippendale highboy top. At first glance the tableau looked real: there were cars and buses on the street, and people on the sidewalk; the neighboring buildings were shown, just as they really are, and casting shadows, just as they do. Unfortunately, because Madison Avenue is so narrow, it is a view that can never be experienced, not unless several buildings on the opposite side of the street were to be demolished to clear the required vista.

Renderings that show buildings in three dimensions are drawn according to the inflexible laws of perspective. But to construct them, the draftsman is free to choose the place from which he will observe the building. He can locate this so-called vantage point at will, even if in the real world it is a spot from which the building is invisible. By shifting the imaginary vantage point, the draftsman has at his disposal the combined equivalent of X-ray vision and a wide-angle lens; he can show a project that is situated on a cramped site, like the AT&T Building, as if it were in a much more open setting.

Drawings can also be cropped and masked. The celebrated renderings of Wright's earliest houses have an arcadian quality that suggests the midwestern plains. No wonder that Europeans, who knew Wright's work only through photographs in books such as the famous anthology published by Wasmuth, thought that they were looking at "prairie houses." In reality, as Brendan Gill has pointed out, their location was distinctly suburban. The most famous example, the Robie house, is on a Chicago street corner, hemmed in today—as it always was, except in Wright's drawings—by less illustrious neighbors.

A drawing can enhance obtrusive reality; the plainest building can be made interesting, charming, or engaging, according to the skill of the draftsman. During the nineteenth century, the Ecole des Beaux-Arts in Paris produced draftsmen of an astonishing, meticulous competence. Their large watercolor drawings depicted every trace of shadow, every swag and marbled surface, every nuance of classical ornament. The paint washes were applied with painstaking care, and the skein of ink lines had a hairlike delicacy. There is a price to be paid for such legerdemain, however. Although the designs vary in quality—and some are very good indeed—it is often difficult to separate the building from its seductive portrayal.

It takes days and weeks to produce drawings of this caliber, and the absorbing work, like all products of craftsmanship, takes on a life of its own. Here is another liability: beautiful drawings can become ends in themselves. Often, if the drawing deceives, it is not only the viewer who is enchanted but also the maker, who is the victim of his own artifice. Alberti understood this danger and pointed out that architects should not try to imitate painters and produce lifelike drawings. The purpose of architectural drawings, according to him, was merely to illustrate the relationship of the various parts. He preferred scale models that could be viewed from different sides and easily altered—that is, played with. But he warned his readers that the building game (although he did not call it that) could deceive. "The making of curious, polished models, with the delicacy of painting, is not required from an architect," he wrote. Models should be "plain and simple, more to be admired for the contrivance of the inventor, than the hand of the workman." Alberti understood, as many architects today do not, that the rules of drawing and the rules of building are not one and the same, and mastery of the former does not ensure success in the latter.

The drawings that Palladio prepared for his *Four Books* followed Alberti's dictum. Maybe it was woodblock technology that imposed a severe restraint on his draftsmanship, but I don't think so. The single-line sketches were intended to convey certain specialized information (such as dimensions) and to indicate general architectural ideals, not to depict the designer's full intentions. There is only one per-

spective drawing in Palladio's book, and it is of a bridge—
the buildings are always primly depicted in plan or in frontal
view, devoid of any surroundings. The sensual materiality
of the Villa Rotonda, the wonderful light within the
churches, and the eloquent siting of the country houses were
essential ingredients of his designs, but they had to be experienced in situ.

The buildings of Le Corbusier rejected the language of
classicism; but when it came to drawing, the Modernist
architect demonstrated what amounted to Albertian restraint. His sketches were crude, like cartoons, although he
was trained as an engraver and was proficient in drawing.
Materials were suggested by jagged cross-hatching or coarse
splatters of dots; trees resembled kidney-shaped coffee tables on spindly wire trunks; the human figures were lumpy
stuffed dolls. These austere drawings and roughly made
models challenged the viewer and they were clearly intended for the atelier, not for the exhibition room.

I can still remember my visit to the Cité Universitaire,
in Paris, to see the residence for Swiss students, a building
designed by Le Corbusier in 1930. Fully grown trees ob-
scured the building, a small four-story slab that was supported on short columns and straddled a low pavilion
containing a common room and a lobby. I had never seen
the building before; but, like most architecture students, I
had pored over the *Oeuvre complète*—an eight-volume record of the architect's lifework—and I could reproduce the
plan of this and other buildings from memory. Which was
all the more reason that the firsthand experience of this
familiar design came as such a surprise. The curved and
angled lobby walls that looked so simple in plan created
unexpectedly complicated spaces. The exterior supports

were like plump tree trunks; the interior columns, inconsequential dots on the drawings, were unusually positioned—several inches from a wall, or penetrating a bookcase. The drawings had not prepared me for the bare, unfinished concrete with visible shuttering marks, and the rough, rubble wall of the common room—this was the beginning of Le Corbusier's so-called Brutalist period— or for the unusual colors of the painted ceilings and ventilating ducts.

What did my own drawings hold in store? Would I be pleasantly surprised when the boatbuilding workshop was finished? Or had I been deceiving myself with my endless sketches of little sheds and barns? It was a year and a half since I had started the design, and throughout the intervening period I had immersed myself in its paper existence. This was an attenuated reality, not purely imaginary but not altogether material either. It was time to stop sketching. In any case, by building the concrete slab I had committed myself, and it was too late to go back.

Once I had decided on the barnlike shape of the building, it was easy to fit the two main functions within it—boatbuilding at one end, living quarters at the other. The latter required a smaller door, and I added a little porch to give some protection from the rain. It was too domestic, and fussy. Instead I made the upper floor overhang the entrance to create a sheltered entry, which looked better. The vestibule lacked light, but a small window would mar the simplicity of the end wall. I put a glass opening in the door instead; now someone answering the door could see the visitor. Big doors for the boat were needed at one end— they had to be in the center—so I put the window above, also in the center. I tried a traditional barn window; the diamond shape looked attractive but would be difficult to open. I made it rectangular, the same proportion as the doors but smaller: now I was following the classic rule of reducing the size of elements as the eye moves up the façade. I made the window at the other end identical, so that as you walked around the building, shapes repeated. But more windows were needed. Too many windows were a problem, however, since the beauty of barns was precisely that they had large blank walls with hardly any fenestration. I made one large window—as big as a barn door—facing south, which could be shared by both upper and lower rooms. A big, long wall and a big window; now it looked better, and it also made the interior seem more spacious. It was cheaper too.

The workroom was at the west end of the building. This meant that the completed boat would have to be maneuvered around the old apple tree, which grew only twenty feet away, on that side of the house. This was hardly an ideal solution, but it seemed never to have occurred to me to locate the workroom at the opposite end. I am not sure why this should have been so. Did I want to sail into the sunset? Or was I unconsciously mimicking the basilican plant of the Dutch barn, which, like churches, had its single door at the west end? Taking the barn as a model had produced not only an uncomplicated building form, and the characteristic two-sloped roof, but also a simple and economic structure. The two long walls carried a series of trussed rafters that spanned the width of the building— sixteen feet—and supported the gable roof. A steep gable roof not only shed water effectively, it also permitted a room on the upper level to be situated not merely under the roof but within it, like an attic. This reduced the height of the external walls and the interior volume of the building, and hence the cost of heating.

To make the tiny living quarters less cramped, I had left a place where one could look down from the upper level; standing below, one was also aware of the sloped ceiling of the attic above. In this way, the sheltering roof—the main architectural element on the exterior—would be experienced within the building, not fully, as in a barn, but at least in fragments. Beauty was not the first consideration in a workshop, but there was no reason that the interior of the little building should not offer a modest measure of pleasure after the long hours of boatbuilding.

A SIMPLE AND ECONOMIC STRUCTURE

٭ ٭ ٭

Building on paper had been an effortless process. A sweep of the eraser was enough to abolish a wall; two darts of the pencil and it reappeared elsewhere. Each fresh page of my sketchbook offered the promise of unlimited, and unexplored, possibilities; each fresh page was an opportunity: "You're not finished yet. There is still time to correct, to change, to improve."

When construction commenced, the two-dimensional plans began to acquire a palpable, three-dimensional presence. Did this mean that the building game was over? No, for even as pencil lines became space, changes could still be made.* Buildings have frequently been modified as a result of the circumstantial discoveries that have taken place during construction. Sometimes changes are the result of an architect's error of judgment, or of inexperience, or of a particularly fortuitous spatial arrangement that has eluded him in the drawings. Or perhaps the sight of the building suggests meliorations to the design. Short of erecting a full-size mock-up on the actual building site, there is sometimes no way to test an architectural idea other than by trying it out.†

Although the architect happily admits last-minute changes and improvements, such improvisation is normally a frustration for the builder, for whom it creates expensive delays. It is also an irritation for the client, who, after all, must pay the extra cost. Happily, in my case, architect, builder, and client were one and the same, and if there was much agonizing and deliberation, there was at least harmony.

As the walls rose, the natural landscape and views of the building made themselves felt. That was when I discovered

---

* "The best friend of the architect is the pencil in the drafting room, and the sledgehammer on the job," Wright said of such changes.

† Clients have usually relied on the architect's rendering to receive an impression of what a building will look like on the building site, but there have been doubting Thomases. A. G. Kroller, a wealthy Dutch industrialist who commissioned the famous German architect Peter Behrens to design a sprawling villa-museum in 1911, had a full-size mock-up of the design built on his country property. Not only was the stage building realistic (it was constructed of wood and canvas painted to simulate fenestration and the actual materials), it was even mobile: steel rails laid on the ground allowed the whole apparatus to be moved back and forth across the site. In the event, Behrens's project was rejected, as were later proposals by such illustrious designers as Mies van der Rohe, Hendrik Berlage, and Henri van de Velde.

that a distant tree blocked what I had thought was a favorable vista, and that the sun didn't quite reach into the room. Nevertheless, I could still change my mind about the size and placement of windows. Partition walls could be put up and taken down; there is still an odd little window in the corner of one room that puzzles the visitor, who does not know that this was once the location of a room containing a toilet.

That such changes were possible was the result of a construction method that was a momentous technological invention of vernacular architecture—the technique of lightweight wood framing. This construction method, which is said to have originated in Chicago in the 1830s, substituted many small wood members for the customary posts and beams of the traditional heavy timber frame. This produced a building as light as a house of cards—the method was first disparagingly called balloon framing or stick building—and like a house of cards, it was made of identical interchangeable, cheap, and expendable parts. These parts—the studs and joists that made up the wall and floor framing—were connected not by chiseled mortise-and-tenon joints, as was a timber frame, but by nails. It was the humble nail that made it possible to join the spindly bits of wood that comprised the frame of a stick building. It was nails, too, that permitted easy changes. It was no complicated matter to pull a nail, to undo a piece of wall, to fill a window, or to reposition a door. There was little waste, as bent nails could be straightened, and leftover short bits of wood were always needed for blocking and bracing.

The popularity of stick building, which now dominates construction in North America, at least for small buildings, was not because of this flexibility alone, however, but was due to another advantage: stick buildings could be built quickly, cheaply, and with little labor. The massive bents of a traditional barn were so heavy that dozens of men were needed to erect them—hence the famous barn-raising bees that were a periodic feature of rural life. The stick builder, on the other hand, manipulated much lighter members; the heaviest floor joist that I had to lift weighed only forty-four pounds. All that was required was a hammer, a saw, a barrel of nails, and a helping hand. I purchased the first three; and Shirley and Vikram—who now found himself inextricably involved in the venture—provided the fourth.

That three people with little experience in construction (Vikram had never even seen a frame building until he came to Canada from his native Gujarat) could undertake such a project was evidence of the most important advantage of stick building—its simplicity. There were only two undemanding operations, cutting and nailing. We built the walls on the concrete slab, which served as a worktable, and tilted them into place. The roof trusses were also assembled on the ground. This was the most rewarding stage in the construction process, since the building took shape quickly, and at the end of each day we could see another piece completed.

I loved this part of the work. Compared with concrete, a nasty, inert material, wood was—or had been—alive. It had a smell and a feel that were pleasurable. So was the rhythm of the framing process, which alternated between the energetic driving of nails into soft pine and the slower and more exacting operations of measuring and cutting. When we stopped, as we did often, the tapping of hammer on nail head and the scraping of saw through wood were replaced by the meadow sounds of birdsong and the chirping of crickets. The natural surroundings heightened the feeling that we were pioneers. So did the fact that we were working with hand tools. There was no electricity on the site, and I had resisted renting a generator. Building by hand was a romantic idea—and one which I would not repeat—but colonists we certainly were. When we were finished, this place, this particular place, would be changed: the meadow would be occupied. It was the reenactment of a primeval process that began with the first hut erected in a forest clearing, and it gave me the feeling of playing out an ancient ritual.

It took us only a few weeks to complete the framing and to nail on the sheathing that braced the spindly studs and joists and turned the skeletal construction into something that resembled a finished building. We laid the asphalt shingles; it was a tedious and unpleasant job, which required balancing precariously on what I now wished were a less steep roof. Vikram had to leave to visit his family, and Shirley and I installed the three windows. The largest one was a good deal heavier than I had expected, but Louise, a friend of Shirley's, dropped in for a visit and was immediately drafted, and the three of us were able to lift the unwieldy frame into place. I nailed up the cedar planks that covered the exterior. By the end of the summer, with the occasional help of other friends, the walls and roof, which architects refer to as the shell, were complete.

All that remained was to finish the inside, work that occupied us during the following summer. The wood-burning stove needed a chimney; the concrete floor had to be painted. I replaced the awkward ladder to the sleeping room with a narrow staircase, which lopped a couple more feet from the workshop area but fortuitously created space for a sitting alcove and a storage cupboard beneath the stair. The living quarters had to be insulated. The unheated workshop was a tall room with a loft at one end; only a pair of wide doors, instead of the sheets of plywood that temporarily secured the opening, were required to complete it.

The building was finished; I was pleased with its appearance. As I had hoped, the general effect was distinctly agricultural and suited the surroundings. The north wall offered a blank face to the public road; a chance passerby would scarcely give it a glance. On the other side, the single large window overlooked the meadow. The cedar boards were rapidly turning gray, and the unobtrusive little barn already looked at home.

⁊⁊ ⁊⁊ ⁊⁊

When a ship is launched, a bottle of champagne is broken against her bow, usually by an important person, and the vessel begins her life. I was looking forward to this ceremony, but that was in the future. We had not performed the *khat muhrat* rite when we started the foundation—much to our later discomfort—and I wanted to make sure that a formal gesture would mark the occasion of completing the building.

There used to be a custom associated with the beginnings of buildings; it concerned laying the first stone. Since stone walls were constructed by starting at the corners and then filling between them, the first stone became known as the cornerstone. It was ceremoniously placed by a prominent personage, whose name and position, together with the date of this auspicious event, were recorded for posterity on the stone's surface. I pass such a stone as I walk to my office. It is at the corner of a university building and, according to the inscription, was laid by the Viscountess Alexander of Tunis on May 29, 1950. The happy combination of Mediterranean names—that of the fabled Macedonian conqueror and that of the ancient Barbary coast seaport—warms the Canadian limestone. The building itself is an undistinguished example in the tepid modernistic style of the postwar period, but its cornerstone has always given me pleasure. It not only marks the passage of time but in a charming way also acknowledges the human endeavor that any building—even an ugly old dowager such as this one—represents.

The cornerstone is also a recognition that there is more to safeguarding the life of a building, and the lives of its inhabitants, than merely solid construction. The stone has a talismanic function similar to that of the white edging that surrounds the doors and windows of Mennonite barns in Pennsylvania, offering protection against incorporeal intruders. Some Mennonite barns are adorned by multicolored, six-pointed stars and whirling swastikas, known locally as hexafoos or witchfeet and intended to protect the cattle within from malfeasance. I have also seen such good-luck swastikas daubed on the walls of humble Hindu slum shanties. Primitive superstition? I am not sure that the governors of my university would admit that they were resorting to the shamanistic protection afforded by the cornerstone when they invited the Viscountess Alexander to the ceremony, but what better patroness to shield against misfortune than the wife of a famous soldier?

There are, of course, no cornerstones in a wood building; but there was a masonry wall in my boatbuilding shed. Flanking the doors of the workroom at its western extremity were two sections of masonry wall, though they were made not of stone units but of glass—well, not exactly glass blocks but bottles: empty wine bottles, gallon jugs, gin and scotch bottles, and four jeroboams safeguarded since our wedding day. Previously, I had spent several years experimenting with inexpensive building materials—sulfur by-products, old tires, tin cans—and although the workshop was built conventionally, this would be at least a token reminder of my earlier obsessions. Anyway, I liked the bottle walls. On the exterior, the ends of the bottles made a pleasant pattern of different-sized circles; on the inside, especially as the sun set, the wall blazed with the amber and emerald colors of several hundred wine and liquor bottles—a bacchanalian rose window.

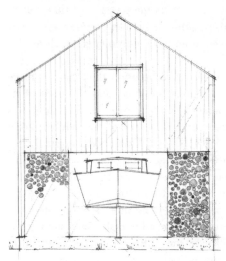

A BACCHANALIAN ROSE WINDOW

The wall of bottles was the last to be built. On the oval brown bottom of an Armagnac bottle I inscribed the date, MCMLXXVII, RYBCZYNSKI FECIT, and the names of my co-workers. It was a corner bottle instead of a stone, and we were commoners all; but it would have to do.

🐝   🐝   🐝

CHRYSALIS

It had taken three years to get this far; in the same period the indomitable Slocum had sailed around the world. If he had been at my shoulder, he would have said impatiently, "Well, you have your workshop—what are you waiting for?" He would have been right, of course—now there were no more excuses, no more putting things off until tomorrow. It was time to begin.

I found the roll of naval blueprints where I had left them, on the top shelf of the bookshelf in my study. The drawings were dusty and starting to yellow, but they still showed a stubby catboat with its broad beam and roomy cockpit. I studied the table of offsets and the lists of materials and familiarized myself once more with the arcane vocabulary of boatbuilding. According to my mentor, Howard Chapelle, the first step was lofting—transferring the dimensions from the drawings to large sheets of paper. In my case, this would provide the full-size templates for the seven frames and the transom that made up the structural skeleton of the hull. The frames themselves were constructed of dimensioned lumber, just like my workshop, although they were mahogany, not pine. The covering was similarly plywood, although of a superior quality and fastened with bronze screws, not common nails.

I should have been in a hurry to begin; but as I commenced these preparations, I realized that although the drawings had not changed, I had. As I read the naval architect's instructions, I imagined myself sawing more wood and pounding more nails. I was surprised to find that I was not looking forward to it. What had previously appeared as a pleasurable pastime was starting to feel like a chore and an obligation. I had to admit, at least privately, that the boatbuilding dream had lost some of its appeal.

Looking back on it, I can see now more clearly what had originally impelled me on this nautical enterprise. The weeks of sawing, fitting, and hammering had been an enjoyable diversion from the intellectual work that normally occupied me. I had needed that change. After years of designing on the drawing table—both as a student and, later, in my practice—I had wanted to build something, anything, with my own hands and with proper tools and real materials; with hammer and nails instead of with an Exacto knife and cardboard, and not in miniature, but full size. This I had done. Unfortunately, as far as boatbuilding was concerned, what had originally attracted me to maritime construction had found fulfillment in landlocked carpentry.

I had constructed a building; but in doing so, I had also discovered that I wanted to convince myself that I was not merely a paper architect, that I could do myself what I had so often delegated to others. This high ideal originated from economic necessity, as it does for most amateur builders; but I found that I enjoyed undertaking each part of the construction process myself. It enabled me to experience the transformation from paper to wood intimately, at first hand. I had also suspected—and in that I was not mistaken—that many architectural discoveries can be made only once a building has been begun, and only by the builder himself.

Now that I had done it, I had to admit to a sense of satisfaction, but also to weariness. Despite the glowing prose of do-it-yourself primers and the initial gratification of seeing the frame rising so rapidly, building on your own over an extended period of time is characterized not only by fulfillment but also by intermittent bouts of depression and anomie. The work drags on; and for every agreeable task, like framing, there is one that is merely drudgery, like installing insulation. Lacking experience, I had made demoralizing mistakes and had to redo work, sometimes several times. Shirley and I grew cranky; we argued. Instead of escaping for weekends to the country, we began to look forward to returning to the city on Sunday night. We took increasingly frequent "vacations" from what came to feel like a never-ending Sisyphean penance.

Our marriage had survived this trial, but I had no desire to test it further. It seemed to me that the boatbuilding would have to be postponed, or even abandoned. When I shamefacedly broached the subject with Shirley, my suggestion was greeted with neither dismay nor exasperation but with cheerful approbation. She had always accepted my boatbuilding scheme with tolerance rather than enthusiasm, and although she didn't actually say, "Finally, you've come to your senses"—at least not immediately—I could see she was relieved. So was I.

ﻩ   ﻩ   ﻩ

If I was not going to build a boat, I obviously didn't need a boatbuilding shed; so what would be the fate of the little barn? We had discussed the eventuality of one day building a house. This possibility had become more real as we spent time in the pleasant rural setting, and as we became involved not only in the construction of the building but also in the first attempts at landscaping and gardening. We were both beginning to realize that the burst of energy that had been released by Vikram's offhanded proposal—"We could do it together"—was not going to be as readily available for future building projects. But maybe there did not need to be any future building. We did not have to add a house to the workshop—we could turn the workshop into a house.

At first, I resisted this notion—it seemed too much like a convenient expediency, a cowardly compromise. On the other hand, I reasoned, if instead of undertaking new construction I converted what we had already built into a dwelling, there would be no more digging, no more pouring concrete, no more manhandling roof trusses and sheets of plywood, no more hoisting rolls of roofing paper and packages of shingles. Instead of building, we would be renovating; it was a tempting thought.

Could it really be done? I examined the possibility of transforming what had been intended as the work area into a kitchen and dining room. There was ample space—the workroom was large enough to accommodate both functions. I would have to add some partition walls and cut out some additional windows, but that was no great problem. Where to put the bathroom? We did not need a two-story-high kitchen, and it did not take long to confirm that if I inserted a floor into the tall room, there would be plenty of space on the upper level for a bathroom. Indeed, my calculations showed that the floor area of the entire building added up to a surprising twelve hundred square feet, which was large enough for a two-bedroom house.

The floor area might be big enough, but at first glance it seemed curious to make one's home in what was essentially a large shed. Of course, humans have improvised their dwellings in all sorts of peculiar situations. I had seen indigent squatters in a Bombay slum who had installed themselves in cardboard packing cases and unused sections of concrete sewer pipes. They remind me of Diogenes, who is said to have lived in a barrel; but he was a hermit making a philosophical point. So was Henry Thoreau, when he built his ten-by-fifteen-foot shed beside Walden Pond. Le Corbusier, who also had an ascetic streak, built a similar-sized cabin in which he and his wife passed their summer holidays. The first structure completed by Thomas Jefferson at Monticello was a tiny one-room cottage—about two hundred square feet in area—which he occupied for four and a half years, first as a bachelor and later as a married man, until the main house was complete.

Compared with these sheds, our situation was palatial, which was just as well, since our house was not intended to be a gesture of ascetic defiance; we definitely wanted a comfortable home, not a temporary shelter. But could this really be achieved in a building that had originally been intended to be a workshop, whose dimensions had been dictated by the size of a boat, and whose form had taken a formal cue from neighboring barns?

By happy accident—this story is full of accidents—the form of my boatbuilding shed was not altogether inappropriate for a house. I had modeled it on the Quebec connected barn and on the cruck barn, and they both shared a common antecedent, one that had a long and honorable pedigree as a place of habitation: the Saxon *longa domus,* or longhouse.

Archaeologists have excavated remains of longhouses built as early as the fifth century; and during the Middle Ages longhouses were common throughout northern Europe. As the name suggests, the longhouse was a long and narrow structure, its thatched roof supported by wood or, later, stone walls. Following an ancient practice, the inhabitants of the oldest longhouses shared them with their cattle. In some versions, the byre—called the "bottom end"—was separated from the dwelling by an open passage resembling a breezeway. In others, the two uses were at opposite ends of a single room; sometimes there were partitions to separate the two groups of occupants, sometimes not. In either case, the living quarters were distinguished by little more than the presence of a central hearth.

These types of dual-purpose longhouses persisted until well into the sixteenth century; indeed, they still survive in remote parts of Ireland and Wales—and in Brittany, whence the longhouse migrated to New France, where it was transformed into the connected barn. Life in a long-house was convivial but crude. Eventually, people were unwilling to share their homes with cattle—and with the smells, noises, ticks, and fleas that accompanied them—and animals began to be housed in separate barns. But the form of the longhouse endured, and long, narrow houses became a staple of vernacular domestic architecture throughout northern Europe.

The length of longhouses varied from thirty to as long as ninety feet; it all depended on the wealth of the owner. The width, however, deviated little: most were between fifteen and twenty feet wide. This represented—and still repre-sents—a distance that could be easily and economically spanned by wooden trusses and covered by a gable roof made of thatch or slate tiles or wood shingles—or, as in my case, asphalt shingles. Thatch required steep roofs, which provided the possibility of a useful hayloft. Once the animals were moved out, this attic space, known as the sollar, be-came a second living floor, used mainly for sleeping.

There are several advantages, in addition to structural simplicity, that explain why this type of house survived as long as it did and why it still represents a serviceable pro-totype for a dwelling. In the days before electric light, *all* buildings were either long and narrow or divided into nar-row wings and provided with courts or light wells—the deep building is a modern invention. But even if artificial illumination is available, rooms without natural light, and view, are disagreeable—that is why windowless offices are passed off on junior staff and stenographers. Scarcely more comfortable are exceedingly deep rooms with but a single window, or fenestration in only one wall. As Alexander had pointed out in one of his "patterns," only when natural light comes from at least two sides of a room can glare and harsh contrasts be avoided. A small, square building with many corner rooms satisfies this requirement, and so does a long, narrow building, one room deep, in which light can enter every room from two sides.

The pleasure of a window is a function not only of its proper disposition in the room and of the view that it presents but also of its orientation with respect to the sun. In the Northern Hemisphere, a north window allows an even and clear illumination, an east window lets in the cheerful morning rays, and a west window admits the glowing light of late afternoons. And best of all is the window looking to the south, which, as Alberti wrote, quoting the classical Roman author Martial, receives "a pure sun, and a clear light." In northern latitudes a south window is especially welcome, since it permits the low winter sun to warm the interior. And the easiest way to provide many such windows is to build rectangular buildings that present their long façades to the sun. I was not surprised to discover that the Saxon longhouses were almost always built on the same east-west axis as my boatbuilding shed.

Long and narrow plans had another benefit. If one was sharing one's longhouse with several cows, it was useful to have the animals as far away as possible. Spreading rooms out along a line, instead of clustering them, created physical distances that continue to give the greatest degree of privacy, both visual and acoustic. In my case, it also provided at least one long view down the length of the house, giving an impression of expansiveness to what was otherwise a small space.

It was evident to me that the barn would indeed make a pleasant house; and once the decision was made, all that remained was to implement the changes. The sleeping loft gained a clothes closet and became a bedroom; the small room below was turned into a sitting room, although I would have to sacrifice the alcove at the bottom of the stairs to the bulky hot-water tank. The tall space that had contained the workroom would be transformed into a large kitchen and eating area. The intermediate floor had room enough for a bathroom, lit by a skylight that I cut into the roof. The addition of a closet and a short piece of wall would convert what had been intended to serve as a loft for storing boatbuilding materials into a spare bedroom that I could also use as a study. It would be reached by a gallery, from which I could look down and see the kitchen below. From there I

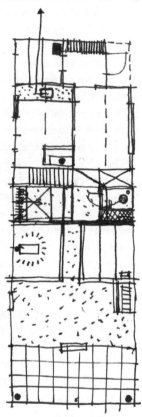

A LONG AND NARROW PLAN

140

could also look out of the new, tall, narrow window—fitted between two studs—that rose from over the sink the full height of the house, and gave a view down the long driveway.

I had left plumbing and electricity until the end. The former proved simpler than I had expected, thanks to plastic fittings and flexible tubing that eliminated the mysteries of soldering and sweating copper pipe. The latter was more problematic. I understood electricity not at all and was obliged to rely on a local electrician, who installed the entry box and placed the wiring. This was only prudent, but I felt sorry to have had to engage a professional; it felt like having a trespasser in the house.

It was two more years before we could move in, for by now we had learned to pace ourselves, and when the work threatened to overwhelm us, we would abandon it for a week or two. As we approached the end, this happened less and less. Eventually, the walls were properly plastered, sanded, and painted, and the sloped ceiling covered in cedar. By the time we were finished, there was little to remind us of the boatbuilding shop except for the opening in the east wall of the kitchen. I had replaced the barn doors with glazed French doors, which could be opened wide, wide enough to move the dining table outside—or wide enough to move a smallish boat inside. But, wiser now, I kept this thought to myself.

(7)

••

THE MIND'S EYE

I had started with a boatbuilding workshop and had finished with a house; I also acquired a client—Shirley.
Earlier she had left me to my own devices, satisfied to aid
me in the construction. This changed. She still helped me,
but now there were questions, objections, demands. It soon
became clear to me that once it was decided that we would
live here, she was not going to put up with improvisation
and make-do solutions. I found myself having to explain
what I was doing and what I was going to do. I had been
able to talk my way around paying clients, but this one
knew me too well. Although I put up a brave, professional
front, the problem was that she was more cognizant of
house design than I was—not of construction but of the
details, of the minutiae of everyday life that constitute
a home.

There was the question of the flooring, for example. In
the kitchen, Shirley wanted a material that would require
little maintenance. Left to her own devices, she would have
opted for something that resembled a car wash and that
could be hosed down once a week. My own concern was
different: I wanted a single material throughout the ground

THE MOST BEAUTIFUL HOUSE

THE SITTING-ROOM ALCOVE

floor. The kitchen and the dining area were combined in one room, and this was connected to the sitting room by a passage but uninterrupted by doors. With different ceiling heights and room volumes, I was counting on a uniform flooring material to tie things together and to give the little house a sense of unity. We might have left the concrete slab as it was—Wright had frequently used waxed concrete floors in his inexpensive houses. But our amateur troweling was too crude to permit the concrete to be exposed; its surface was so flaky and dusty that we had been obliged to paint it the year before. We finally decided on ceramic tile, which could be, if not exactly hosed down, at least mopped,

144

and which would serve equally well in the sitting room and in the kitchen.

The kitchen has become the single most complicated area in a contemporary house. An older house can easily be made habitable with minor alterations to the bedrooms and living rooms, which have changed little over the years; but the kitchen usually requires extensive remodeling. This is only partly for technological reasons, although the presence of dishwashing machines, microwave ovens, and an assortment of appliances must be taken into account. But we also use the kitchen differently. We spend both less and more time in it—that is, we want things to be convenient, but we also want the kitchen to be a part of the house, not an isolated workplace. Hence the blending of dining room and kitchen. This is not so much "eating in the kitchen" as it is "cooking in the dining room."

Traditional kitchen furniture was developed at the turn of the century. Since that time it has consisted of counters with cupboards and drawers below, and shallower cabinets, with shelves, above. The dimensions have become so standardized that I, like all architects, could reel them off without thinking: counters, twenty-four inches deep and thirty-six inches high; cabinets, twelve inches deep, starting eighteen inches above the counter and extending thirty to forty-two inches high. I drew such an arrangement; it was not well received. "Why," asked Shirley, who was unhampered by my professional training, "do kitchens have to be this way?" She explained that she didn't like deep cupboards that required bending down and rummaging around each time a cooking pot was needed. And things stored in tall cabinets were equally inaccessible. "Anyway, why does everything have to be hidden?" When you were cooking—

as we both did—and needed an implement, you wanted to be able to have it immediately to hand. "Why can't a kitchen be designed like a carpentry shop, or a laboratory, where all the tools are out in the open?"

And that is what our kitchen became. The long work top was supported not by solid cupboards but by a fourteen-inch-deep box that did not reach the floor. The box contained drawers, some shallow, for utensils and cutlery, and others as deep as filing cabinets, for appliances and mixing bowls. "The harder the utensils are to see, the less you will use them," counsels Julia Child, so instead of cabinets above the work top, I built a wooden rack on which we could hang pots and pans, knives and spatulas, all the most commonly used tools, as well as supplementary accessories such as a scale, a clock, and the telephone. Old habits are hard to break, however, and I instinctively made the counter twenty-four inches deep. It was a mistake; the inevitable accumulation of toaster, coffee grinder, cookbooks, and other cooking impedimenta suggest that a depth of not less than thirty inches should have been provided.

The other room in which much has changed in recent decades is the bathroom. Here it is not so much a question of technology—that is too grand a word for whirlpool baths—but of attitudes. The conventional bathroom—a walk-in closet with plumbing fixtures—originated in hotels, which may have accounted for its niggardly dimensions. But if it remained tiny in homes, that was not because of economics; in the forties and fifties, even large houses and apartments had small bathrooms. The bathroom was not enlarged because efficiency, not comfort, was the prime consideration. A prudish society considered that bathing was a hygienic necessity, not a pleasure. Big baths and big

bathrooms were for decadent Hollywood stars or for decadent civilizations such as that of ancient Rome.

Another reason that the tiny bathroom persisted is that
ever since Palladio designers have thought of rooms in terms
of standardized shapes and dimensions. Modern reference
books, such as *Architectural Graphic Standards*, depicted
a small number of normative bathroom plans. During the
building game, these model solutions could be introduced
intact into the emerging house plan, if not as an after-
thought, at least without second thought. This is what I
had often done myself in the houses I designed for others.
In the excitement of seeing their future home taking shape
on paper, my clients had usually given little thought to the
detailed layout of the bathroom. This time, the client was
less receptive. "Why is the bathroom so small?" she asked.
I tried to argue that space was at a premium in our small
house, but to no avail. She was insistent. The bathroom
grew until it was twice as large as the conventional five-
by-seven-foot cubicle that I had first drawn.

Shirley favored showers and I preferred baths. Neither
of us liked showering in a bathtub—it always reminded me
of Alfred Hitchcock's *Psycho*. However, if I included both
a shower stall and a tub, the room would feel as cramped
as before, so I was prepared to compromise. When Shirley
suggested she wanted tiles on the walls, and ceiling, if possible, I remembered a design for a bathroom (I think it was
by Le Corbusier) in which a small cubicle, only five feet
square, contained a sink, a water closet, and a shower.
There was no shower stall; instead, all exposed surfaces
were tiled and the floor sloped to a drain. This is a common,
space-saving solution on boats, which is probably where Le
Corbusier encountered it. It would work even better in a

larger room—at least the toilet seat would stay dry—and it would feel as spacious as the echoing public showers of my school days.

With the amicable resolution of these and many smaller issues, the house took shape—or, rather, changed internally, for the exterior appearance remained much as before. But here also the client had a request. She communicated it obliquely, more by implication than by direct statement, but I sensed that she was dissatisfied with the exterior aspect of the house. A shed was all right for boatbuilding, but she expected something more of a home. Commodity, firmness, and delight had been satisfied, but something else was missing. The little barn fitted in—and yet it didn't fit.

ﻬ   ﻬ   ﻬ

The appearance of buildings is obviously an important consideration for architects: the aim is to achieve not only beauty and grace but also propriety. "What a disagreeable and unseemly thing would it be, if in a very large fabric there should be small halls and rooms; and, on the contrary, in a little one, there should be two or three rooms that took up the whole," counseled Palladio. Propriety, or decorum, as he called it, was affected not only by a building's size but also by its use. Alberti and Vitruvius likewise distinguished broadly between buildings designed for necessity, for convenience, and for pleasure, and also between buildings for different levels of society—for the poor as well as for the rich. According to them, buildings for different purposes should not only be planned differently, they should also look different.

The first architectural writer to single out houses as the subject of a separate study was Sebastiano Serlio, a contemporary of Michelangelo. His unpublished treatise on domestic design was a catalog of every sort of home, ranging from an enormous royal palace to modest town houses. The difference between these structures lay not merely in their size and in the variety of spaces provided but also in the architectural treatment of the façades. That of the king's residence, *magnifica et grande,* was replete with several superimposed classical orders; the tiny one-room "house for a poor artisan" had no façade decoration, although it did sport a Serlio trademark, an ornamented chimney. It was a similar sense of propriety that influenced Wright in the Fallingwater house. Its structural flamboyance was predicated on its use as a rural weekend retreat for a wealthy couple and would have been out of place in a middle-class, suburban family home such as the decorous Jacobs house, which he designed a year later.

Differences in appearance are even more marked if one contrasts public and utilitarian buildings. A library has traditionally displayed a different level of architectural rhetoric than, say, a warehouse. This is not a question of function, since both buildings are, in a sense, places for storage. But a library is supposed to look like a library—that is, it should reflect society's attitude toward books, learning, and knowledge. The same attitude underlies the many neo-Gothic buildings that were built on North American campuses at the turn of the century. Although most of the activities of a university department can be efficiently housed in a conventional office building, the ornamented piles of granite and limestone were, if not original, at least a recognition that scholarship deserved a different setting than commerce.

How buildings look and what buildings look *like* are not the same thing. In 1969, President Georges Pompidou of

France decided to build a national cultural center to house, display, and celebrate the contemporary arts. This ambitious project included not only a museum of modern art (relocated from another site) but also a new public library, a center of industrial design, cinemas, theaters, and a laboratory for progressive music and acoustic research. An international architectural competition was announced, and attracted more than six hundred entries. The competition program made it clear that the building was not to be merely a museum of contemporary art and design but a distinctly modern museum, "aimed towards a vast public," housed in an "architectural and urban complex which will mark our century." The use of terms such as "experimental," "dynamic," and "imaginative" underlined the desire for something new and startling.

New and startling was what they got—even before the building was completed, eight years later, it had become the subject of a bitter controversy. Some of the debate was the inevitable result of building a huge—one million square feet—new structure in the middle of Paris. Many people were uncomfortable with President Pompidou's popularizing attitude to culture ("a supermarket for the arts," a newspaper columnist huffily called it), and it was a humbling blow to national pride that the prizewinning architects were an Englishman and an Italian. Once construction began, these issues receded, however, and most of the critical comments focused on the building's appearance.

The cultural center was located in the Marais, a historic residential district in the center of the city. The new building made no concession to its gray stone neighbors, however—it was entirely of steel and glass. Like the Farnsworth house, it was a rectangular glass box, although it was a much bigger box, ten stories high and almost six hundred feet long. Its structure was exposed, and painted white, like its predecessor's, but there the similarity ended. Mies's house, like all his designs, was monochrome; the Paris museum was a riot of bright colors. Mies was sober; this building was lighthearted: the orange air-intakes for the parking garage resembled a ship's ventilators, and the principal façade was to have been covered with neon signs, giant TV screens, and electronic billboards in the manner of Times Square. Mies decorously concealed the domestic utilities and mechanical spaces in a service core covered with book-matched primavera wood; here nothing was hidden and everything was revealed, nor did the museum incorporate any of the materials traditionally associated with prestigious public buildings.

According to its architects, the building that came to be called the Centre Pompidou "reveals its internal mechanism to all who look up at it. It is a flexible, functional, transparent, inside-out building." The structure of giant trusses was carefully exposed to display how the building was built. The glazed escalators were suspended on the exterior to show how people circulated through the building, just as the blue air-conditioning ducts that snaked up the façade revealed the movement of fresh, cooled, and stale air. The freight elevators, painted bright red, were not buried inside the core of the building but moved up and down on the exterior.

Inside-outness was the rule of this building game—the designers described the building as a giant Meccano set— and it was intended to convey an atmosphere of play, excitement, and fun. To the layman, who was understandably less fascinated by the inner workings of buildings than the builders, the mammoth assemblage of crisscrossing steel trusses, exposed air-handling equipment, and colored pipes and ducts suggested a different image altogether. "Is this a museum?" fumed one critic in *Le Monde*. "This garage, this gasworks, this petroleum refinery?"

Was this merely Gallic sour grapes? I don't think so. Many people were genuinely perplexed by the unusual design; others found the juxtaposition of pipes and paintings offensive. Of course, the architects of the Centre Pompidou had not intended to imply a parallel between cracking crude oil and viewing art. Their purpose was not to mock museum culture but to display "honestly" how a building was assembled. They were concerned with the quality of construction, and the sophisticated design had none of the roughness of an industrial building. The exposure of mechanical services, the articulation of functional requirements, and the expression of structure had a pedagogic function.

The ideals that produced the Centre Pompidou grew out of the architectural manifestos of the 1920s—a period that espoused a machinelike architecture for a Machine Age— and were the underpinnings of what became known as the Modern Movement. In its time, it too had outraged the public; when it first appeared in France, the white, flat-roofed architecture was often described as *arabe,* which was far from praise. Today, the style that provoked such racist epithets has become an accepted fashion for the villas of the wealthy, not only on the Riviera but also in the Hamptons. It is possible that the Centre Pompidou too will outlive its critics' outrage. After all, the Tour Eiffel, whose construction was loudly decried by many contemporary artists, including Zola and Maupassant, has become a cherished symbol of the city of Paris, just as beloved as Eiffel's earlier tower the Statue of Liberty, although the lady with the torch was popular from the beginning.

Whatever the outcome, the controversy engendered by such buildings as the Centre Pompidou touches on an important aspect of architecture. We do eventually get used to all buildings—we have no choice; they are too big and too permanent to ignore—but that does not mean that all buildings will gain our affections. People expect buildings not only to function, to be structurally solid, and to fit into their surroundings but also to conform to what is proper and fitting. That is why the Centre Pompidou upset so many people. It was not that Parisians disliked oil refineries but that the extravagant industrial imagery of the building suggested a glorification of the technical world that seemed to many of them to be at odds with the creative arts and with museums.* Instead of a lesson in building science, they saw a building that looked like a factory.

Experiencing buildings in terms of metaphors is not unusual. The arched white roofs of the Sydney Opera House have been described as sails, or seashells, just as the curves of the roof of Le Corbusier's chapel at Ronchamp remind many observers of a nun's wimple. The nicknames that buildings acquire are often metaphorical. The CBS corporation's New York headquarters looks like a solid dark chunk of granite, and its (ominous) appellation is Black Rock. The term "Pentagon," which describes the American military establishment, is derived from the shape of the five-sided building in which the Department of Defense is

---

* It should also be noted that the Centre Pompidou, with glass walls, deep galleries, and no overhead natural light, is a poor environment for enjoying works of art.

housed. Not far away is another building with a famous metaphorical description—the White House.* Some metaphors can be cruel. Ask a Roman the way to *la torta nuziale*—the wedding cake—and he will immediately know that you mean the Vittorio Emanuele Monument, a bombastic marble confection built in 1885 to commemorate the reunification. The forbidding government building that houses the office of the premier of Quebec has an exaggerated regard for security that has earned it the scornful sobriquet *le bunker*. There is a Montreal hotel with rows of scalloped, semicircular bay windows, which I have several times heard called "the cheese grater." Students at the University of Toronto refer to their library, a forbidding bastion with tiny windows, as "Fort Book."

It sounds strange to speak of metaphor—or meaning—with respect to architecture. After all, buildings do not really speak to us the way books or movies do; architecture is not *about* anything, it *is* something, the same way that a chair is a chair, or a table, a table.

Or is it? Buildings can carry complex messages. I used to frequent a Montreal tavern that belonged to a retired professional athlete. The entrance was through a dark vestibule in which were a pair of swing doors. Instinctively, you placed your hand against the push plate, but instead of the usual metal you encountered a series of small black rubber disks. The sensation was unexpected, but the rubber

---

* The White House—which is a copy of an Irish ducal country seat—was originally known as the Presidential Palace; Madison called it the Executive Mansion. It was only after 1814 that its gray stone walls were painted white to mask the effects of a destructive wartime fire. Coincidentally, the home of the Argentinean president, in Buenos Aires, is called the Casa Rosada, or Pink House.

disks were somehow familiar—of course, hockey pucks! The retired sportsman was Henri Richard, a hockey player (nicknamed the "Pocket Rocket," the younger brother of the renowned Maurice). The connotation, however, was not merely one of sport, and hence manliness, and beer drinking; the wit of using an iconic sports object in an unusual setting also implied something slightly offbeat— this was one retired jock who was not asking to be taken altogether seriously. The tavern door presaged more athletic metaphors inside: a suspended ceiling fabricated entirely from hockey sticks, and barred wall niches, as in a pilgrimage church, but containing different relics—ice skates and old Canadiens uniforms.

Is this the language of architecture: literary allusion and visual punning? It certainly was in the past. Classical buildings, which today, for most people, carry merely vague connotations of antiquity or monumentality, originally incorporated precise meanings. To the ancient Greeks, what we now refer to as decoration was much more than embellishment. The architectural historian George Hersey has suggested that "temples were read as concretions of sacrificial matter, of the things that were put into graves and laid on walls and stelai. This sense of architectural ornament is very different from the urge to beauty." He gives many examples. The egg-and-dart molding recalled the eggs that were used in temple ceremonies and also sold to visitors. The triglyphs and metopes that constituted the entablature of a Doric temple suggested sacrificial animal parts; the *guttae,* or drops, beneath the triglyphs (thighs) represented the sacred fluids that were drained onto the altar. Eating, an important part of the sacrifice, was suggested by the entablature (table) and by the rows of dentils (teeth) that surrounded it, immediately beneath the cornice. The triangular area at the gable end, which was filled with sculptural bas-relief, was called a tympanum, after the structure of bones and animal skin that was used as a drum but could also double as a sacrificial table.*

Columns, which were the building blocks of classical architecture, are generally assumed to have originated as tree trunks—a built metaphor for the sacred groves in which the ancient Greeks conducted their religious sacrifices. But they had human connotations also, sometimes explicitly, as in caryatids—human figures used as columns—and sometimes by allusion. The flutes, which referred to rods or spear shafts, also suggested the folds of clothing; the capital was a headdress; the base, a foot. And the general proportions were intentionally human. The classical orders later acquired other meanings. For succeeding centuries, the Tuscan order connoted rural homeliness and practicality; Inigo Jones used the Tuscan order in Saint Paul's to indicate frugality, which is what led Walpole to liken the church to a barn. Doric suggested sturdy masculinity; femininity was symbolized by the acanthus-leaved Corinthian column, which according to Wotton was "lasciviously decked like a courtesan . . . Corinth having been one of the wantonest towns in the world." The more restrained Ionic was used in buildings where a matronly or scholarly appearance was called for. The fifth order, the Composite, which had been documented first by Alberti, was the most extravagant: a combination of Ionic and Corinthian.

---

* The relationship between temple ornament and sacrificial rites was suggested not only by visual forms but by puns, homonyms, and other verbal associations. Hersey refers to this as "troping."

Alberti and his contemporaries considered buildings equally on the intellectual and on the material plane. For example, the many centralized buildings they designed were built metaphors for the literary, humanist notion of man as the center of the universe. The Renaissance public likewise experienced palazzos and churches not only as rich visual forms but as physical embodiments of literary ideas. Such ideas became another way of perceiving buildings, not only visually but in the imagination, thanks, mainly, to memory.

Throughout the Middle Ages, scholars used a variety of mnemonic systems as aids in retaining information; this was an important skill in times when many could not read and when books were, in any case, rare. The origin of these mnemonic systems, which survived until the Renaissance, was ancient; but what is curious is that most were based on buildings. "In order to form a series of places in memory," wrote Quintilian, the first-century-A.D. Roman author of a widely read book on oratory, "a building is to be remembered, as spacious and varied a one as possible, the fore-court, the living room, bedrooms, and parlors, not omitting statues and other ornaments with which the rooms are decorated." This personal memory bank, or memory house, was then furnished and decorated in ways that would recall the information that was being memorized. A house dedicated to remembering the colors of the spectrum—to suggest a trivial example—could have a red front door, an orange floor mat, a yellow hallway, and so on. Using such devices, the skilled practitioner could retain large numbers of images. The sixteenth-century Jesuit missionary Matteo Ricci was said to have been able to recall up to five hundred random Chinese ideograms and then repeat the list in reverse order. Depending on how much was to be remembered, the memory images could be contained in a house, a palace, or even a town.

In analogous fashion, the physical layout of ancient towns was a repository for memory. The surveyors of Roman colonial settlements characteristically laid out the streets in an orthogonal pattern. These towns resembled a modern suburban subdivision, an unrelieved grid of intersecting streets, and they have been described as simply expanded army camps. But there was more to these plans than functional or military necessity: they reflected the Roman citizen's view of the cosmos. The town was divided into four quarters by two main, intersecting streets: the *cardo* (the solar axis) and the *decumanus* (the line of the equinox). As historian Joseph Rykwert put it, "The Roman who walked along the *cardo* knew that his walk was the axis round which the sun turned, and that if he followed the *decumanus,* he was following the sun's course. The whole universe and its meaning could be spelt out of his civic institutions—so he was at home in it."

Hindu builders also developed an elaborate technique for overlaying an imaginary memory-diagram over the building site. According to the *Manasara,* the building plot, whether it was to receive a single building or an entire town, was to be divided into a checkerboard of squares, the exact number depending on its size and type. Each of the squares was assigned to one of the pantheon of Hindu deities: the four corners, for example, were given over to the four demon goddesses, Charagi, Vidarika, Putana, and Rakshasi; the central square belonged to Brahma. Superimposed on this grid, which resembled the Roman *castrum,* was the body of the presiding deity of the site, with his navel in the exact center of the site, his head in the central square of the east side, and his hands and feet oriented in particular directions. The center of the town—or of the house, for the method applied to both—was the place of Brahma, and the center of being of the site-deity.

The influence of such cosmic surveying continued for a long time. In 1727, when Maharajah Sawai Jai Singh decided to build a new capital city for his kingdom of Jaipur, he sent his architects and planners abroad, to visit England and France. He must not have been impressed with their reports, for his new city took neither Belgravia nor Versailles as a model. Instead, its elegant plan was based on the *vastu-purush* mandala, a sacred Hindu symbol, magnified to urban proportions. In 1986, when a new city for one hundred thousand persons was being planned on the outskirts of Jaipur, its planner, Balkrishna Doshi, consciously based his design on many of the concepts established by his predecessor.

The existence of a mythical city superimposed on the real thing seems farfetched to us. But we have our own urban memory-diagrams. When we say "on the other side of the tracks," "Main Street," or "the red-light district," we are referring to both a physical place and an idea. In the 1850s, Americans began to say "downtown" to denote the main business district, although only in a few cities, such as San Francisco and Montreal, was the business area really lower than the rest of the city. Indeed, the phrase had nothing to do with topography, for it originated on the flat island of Manhattan, where the business district, at the south end of the city, was always depicted at the bottom of the city map. Hence, "the Bronx is up and the Battery's down." By coincidence, in many cities "uptown" also meant the most fashionable residential area, which really was higher, since only the wealthy could afford to build on inaccessible heights.

Although Montreal does have homes of the wealthy located on the slopes of Mount Royal, and a real downtown, there is no "uptown"; instead, east and west have long been the chief coordinates of the city. In its infancy, east represented the past, the mother country, and west was the future, the unknown frontier. In its commercial heyday, the island-city was a great transport center, exchanging wheat from the west for immigrants from the east. The East End and West Island also came to characterize its double ethnic origins: the sun rose on neighborhoods that were traditionally French and working-class and set on their English, middle-class counterparts. Like the Roman, the Montrealer walking along his *decumanus*—Sherbrooke Street—knew well his position along the line that stretched between the two poles of language, class, and affluence. Indeed, so strong has this cultural orientation become that it ignores the inconvenient fact that like most of the so-called east–west streets in the city, Sherbrooke Street is out of alignment with the course of the equinox. Its nineteenth-century surveyors paid little attention to the sun; the Romans would have been more careful.

A poorly laid out building is often called a rabbit warren or a maze, suggesting that there is no evident structure in the plan, no mental model. But not any model will do; it has to be simple enough to grasp and remember. For centuries, the plans of classical buildings, large and small, have been informed by the geometry of the human body—axiality, frontal symmetry, head and arms, front and back. The front door (a sort of mouth) was in the center of the front façade (face), and one entered a grand hall (the trunk of the body) on two sides of which the arms, called wings (to mix the metaphor), extended. The anthropomorphism of architectural descriptions—we still refer to a building's spine, or heart, or even bowels—underlines the persistence of the body model.

Such conveyance of meaning by architectural forms is possible because people experience buildings not only as volumes and forms to be seen—the "masterly, correct and magnificent play of masses brought together in light," as Le Corbusier's famous definition would have it—but also intellectually, in the mind's eye.

ఌ   ఌ   ఌ

The symbolic meaning of architecture can be profound, as it is in the case with places of worship and important public monuments. But the language of buildings can also convey more mundane messages: where to go, what is important, how the building is to be used. It is easiest to discern this function if it is absent or if it is misinterpreted. The stock scene in movie comedies in which a flustered visitor wishing to leave a strange home finds himself in the clothes closet illustrates precisely such a confusion. Like all humor, it is an exaggeration of the familiar; we have all had frustrating encounters with doors—not only identifying the right one but opening it once we have found it. There is a bank entrance that I go through frequently but which always manages to confound me. The door is made of plate glass, and its pristine beauty is unsullied by visible hinges or pillars; the elegant handle extends the full width of the door. I always have a small struggle going through that door— sometimes I pull instead of push, sometimes I push against the hinge. I feel like taping a sign to the door—PUSH HERE.

We usually think of signs as being written—FIRE EXIT or TRADESMEN'S ENTRANCE—but the visual clues present in architectural forms are also signs. Unlike written signs, however, architectural objects usually convey several messages at once. A brass object located in the center of the door at roughly eye level signals "door knocker." If it is shaped like a hunting dog, it also suggests "country house" or simply "old-fashioned." The vertical metal plate that protects a door's surface from excessive wear and tear signals that this is a swinging door, and that the plate is the place against which to push. At the same time, if the plate is made of a precious material such as plated silver or ivory, it also conveys a sense of wealth and prestige; it would be natural to presume that such a door leads to somewhere— or someone—important. In that sense, Louis Sullivan's famous dictum "Form follows function" could be recast as "Form follows function, but it also *designates* function."

Umberto Eco has described the different symbolic properties of architectural objects as fulfilling either a primary or a secondary sign-function. The first is denotive and related directly to the utilitarian function of the object; the second category is connotative and carries a more complex set of meanings. The primary sign-function of a push plate, for example, is to denote how to open the door; the connotations of prestige are secondary. According to Eco, neither category is fixed, and over time one or the other can change or even disappear. Keys and locks had great symbolic meaning in the past—something that they have largely lost today, except in the charming ceremony of presenting a distinguished visitor with the key to the city. On the other hand, although the door knocker has lost its utilitarian function to the electric buzzer, it continues to be used for its secondary, connotative meaning. Similarly, the primary function of such elements as window shutters, chandeliers, and fireplaces has taken second place to their largely symbolic use as signs of home and domesticity.

Thanks to the influence of writers such as Eco, as well as of the French critic Roland Barthes, the science of semiology enjoyed a brief period of fashion among architectural theoreticians. Its impact on practitioners was slight, however. Most architects were interested in inventing new and original forms; and, as Eco himself admitted, whereas written and spoken language was characterized by flexibility and could be manipulated to produce a wide variety of messages, architectural signs were relatively limited in their capacity to provide novel meanings. If architects were to accept the idea that buildings were collections of signs, this could mean that in order for the public to "read" their designs, they would have to use familiar and traditional forms; this most avant-garde designers were unwilling to do.

Hence the lukewarm response that many modern buildings receive from the public, which literally does not "understand" them. Both the client and the architects of the Centre Pompidou withstood public pressures to alter the building. The architects of the Hongkong and Shanghai Bank, on the other hand, had to bend to the demands of *feng-shui*, but the popular reaction to the appearance of this building has also been ambivalent. Although this skyscraper displays a gravity that is appropriate for a major bank—no blue pipes and red elevators here—the Chinese businessmen I met did not admire the building. What seemed to me to be a sophisticated example of the latest building technology—the built equivalent of an expensive German sedan—did not live up to their expectations. Here was the most expensive office building in the world, but it simply did not look to them like a place to keep money. Or, rather, since this was a materialistic, commercial city, it did not look like a place that celebrated the accumulation of wealth. Its pristine but impersonal details and its monochromatic, self-effacing, battleship-gray exterior left them cold. I suspected that they much preferred a nearby tower that was covered in gold-anodized aluminum and gleamed in the tropical sun like a thirty-story bar of bullion.

ya   ya   ya

What had disturbed Shirley was that our home didn't "look like a house." The long, simple volume with its gray wood walls was unmistakably a barn. It lacked the familiar signs of habitation, such as porches, shutters, or distinctive chimneys (there *was* a chimney, but it was inconsequential). The gable roof was unbroken by dormers; indeed, the severe north wall—now the "front" of the house—contained only two windows, and one of these was a tall narrow slot, not homey at all.

The utilitarian appearance of the building was eventually softened by a screened porch, which we added after the first summer of flies and mosquitoes, and by the slowly maturing garden. These domestic appurtenances helped, but they were not enough. Eventually I realized that what was conspicuously absent in our house was a front door. When the building had still been a workshop, I

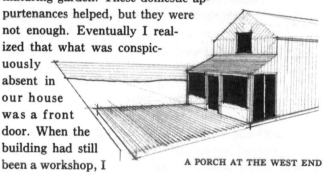

A PORCH AT THE WEST END

had located a door at the east end, but facing south, to shelter it from the prevailing northwesterly winds. This serviceable "back door" was now the main entrance, which meant that it was invisible to anyone approaching the house.

The front door has always been a place of great symbolic importance. Ever since men lived in caves, the front door—and its threshold—have demarcated the transition between inside and outside, between safety and danger, between the public and the private worlds. We angrily show people the door, or considerately we walk them to it; we knock on the door and wait to be invited in. It is the place for many everyday ceremonies of arrival and departure, for familial hugs and for furtive, adolescent goodnight kisses. It is the memory of these that gives front doors personality—that is why we adorn them with Christmas wreaths and Thanksgiving corn.

The importance of a clearly visible front door, then, is only incidentally to orient the visitor; that, as Eco would say, is its primary sign-function. Its secondary purpose, which has become predominant, is connotative and symbolic: it celebrates arrival and departure; it is a sign of welcome as well as an acknowledgment of the vulnerable breach in the inviolable boundary of the domestic sphere. It signals "home."

Front doors were traditionally located in prominent positions—usually the precise center of the façade. Since a door is a relatively small architectural element, an enlarged surround was usually added to give it a greater visual presence. If the house was a grand residence, then further emphasis could be given to the entrance by interrupting the wall at this point with either a recess or a projection. In the east front of the Louvre, which is several hundred feet long, the presence of the entrance is signaled by a protruding central bay, surmounted by a pediment whose tympanum is filled with a bas-relief showing the regal coat of arms of the owner. A columned portico was another way of identifying the door; in a Palladian country house, the portico is visible from a great distance as one approaches along the tree-lined allée.

These are the solutions of classical architecture, but they are remarkably durable—they still speak to us. They reappear in the smallest suburban bungalow and in the most mediocre mobile home. Here, the domestic entrances make do with smaller-scale versions of classical devices: porches, raised galleries, decorated frames. A pair of concrete figures flanks the steps; turned columns support the roof. If possible, the front door continues to be placed in the center of the façade.

So powerful is the front-door sign that many rural houses in Quebec, and elsewhere, have front doors that are rarely used—in some cases so rarely that there is not even a pathway leading to them. Like that of the traditional parlor, their secondary sign-function has become dominant; the door is opened only for weddings and funerals. The front-door sign transcends cultural bounds. I have seen slum shanties in India and in Africa, mud-plastered hovels without even a window but whose doors were treated to a painted edging, a moving sign of human occupation.

I could have painted a counterfeit front door on the wall of our house, which might have improved its appearance but would have been a disabled symbol—like a knocker that couldn't knock or a chimney out of which smoke never curled. The opportunity to do something about the front door came a year after we had moved. I was spending more and more time writing, and I needed a proper study. We also lacked a place where we could store dry firewood and keep tools, ladders, a lawn mower, and the other accessories of country living. I extended the house sixteen feet to the east. On the ground floor, an unheated woodshed was separated from the house by a breezeway; the study was above.

I moved the front door so that it opened into the breezeway. But the breezeway alone was not enough to signal "house." Its square opening could be mistaken for the open drive-through of an English barn. I built a small portico that protruded from the long north wall. I was too much of a modernist to introduce a classical order—Tuscan would have been appropriate—but the posts added a human scale to the long façade. The portico was what architects call a "transition space," not quite inside, not altogether outside—a place to greet visitors and exchange final goodbyes. The portico roof was translucent plastic, which, in the evening, glowed like a giant lamp. It was a comforting sight as one came down the long drive. "Welcome home," it said.

THE MOST BEAUTIFUL
HOUSE IN THE WORLD

THE verb "to habit" combines three seemingly discon-
nected meanings. It signified (for it is no longer in common use) to dress, or clothe; it also indicated the act of
dwelling in, or inhabiting; lastly, it meant to accustom, or
familiarize. Although the verb is antiquated, its deriva-
tives—a nun's habit, a habitation, a bad habit—endure.
What do garments, dwellings, and customs have in common, other than the Latin root of "habit"? The sense development of this root, according to the *Oxford English
Dictionary,* began with *habere,* to have or hold—whence
holding oneself, or showing oneself to the outside world.
This could be accomplished externally, by one's demeanor
or bearing and, by extension, one's dress and even by one's
house, or else internally, in mind, through one's comport-
ment, which led to the sense of familiar or customary
behavior.

The oldest sense of "habit," at least in the English language (in which the word derived its many meanings, at
different times, from French as well as from Latin), had to
do with attire. The connection between dress and habitation
is obvious—our homes, like our clothes, both protect and

169

adorn us. I have seen African houses that resemble hats and are made out of similar material. And like clothes, houses tell a great deal about us, about our social status, our attitudes, and our way of life.

When Goethe visited the Villa Rotonda, he was moved to note in his diary: "Never, perhaps, has art accomplished such a pitch of magnificence." This was the building seen through an artist's eyes. Someone else might have seen a tile-roofed and stucco-walled north Italian farmhouse, draped with classical porches and judiciously clothed with the sparsest decoration. Seen this way, the villa represented the pragmatic Renaissance attitude toward antiquity: beautiful, yes, but also a building that was the product of a particular time and place.

The client who had commissioned Palladio to build the hilltop villa was Monsignor Paolo Almerico, a retired ecclesiastic. After a long career as a papal adviser in Rome, he had acquired a taste for classical architecture and the acumen to recognize the budding architectural talent of a native Vicenzan. Did he also have a taste for the good life? The villa has been described as a place of entertainment, and it does have the air of a pleasure pavilion about it. It is easy to imagine the monsignor standing in the portico, warmed by the morning sun streaming between the Ionic columns and enjoying the view of the cultivated slopes that surrounded his home.

Happily, this is an experience that the modern visitor can share, for the current owners of the Villa Rotonda permit the public to see the grounds. On those days, however, the house is closed, and despite the well-kept gardens it appears unoccupied—it looks like a beautiful sarcophagus, an effect that is heightened by the sculpted human figures that stand like funerary sentinels on the pediments of the porticoes and flanking the stairs. One wishes to have seen the house when it was not a revered monument but a bustling home, with bedding being aired out the windows and bags of produce piled up in the porticoes (the upper story was used as a grain loft), with the smell of cooking coming from the ground-floor kitchen, and with the bustle of life disturbing, and enlivening, its pristine beauty.

"Inhabiting" does not only mean living within. It means occupying—infusing a particular site with our presence, and not only with our activities and physical possessions but also with our aspirations and dreams. We live in a house, and in the process we make it alive. Samuel Clemens wrote of his Hartford home: "Our house was not unsentient matter—it had a heart and a soul, and eyes to see with; and approvals and solicitudes and deep sympathies; it was of us, and we were in its confidence and lived in its grace and in the peace of its benedictions. We never came home from an absence that its face did not light up and speak out in eloquent welcome—and we could not enter it unmoved."

Writers, whose homes are usually also their workplaces, frequently give identity to—and are identified with—their dwellings. So it is with the houses that belonged to Kipling, Faulkner, and Hemingway. But Clemens's sentimental affection for his home was not only that of a householder but also that of a house builder. The nineteen-room mansion at 351 Farmington Avenue in Hartford, Connecticut, had been designed for the Clemens family by Edward Tuckerman Potter, a New York architect. The house was extravagant and idiosyncratic—a showy concoction of gingerbread Gothic, turreted, chimneyed, and gabled on all sides, its polychrome brickwork accented with black and vermilion. An ivy-covered porch ran along the front of the house, terminating in a covered outdoor room, the "ombra." From the sheltered carriageway, the visitor entered a grand hall that led to the library, which opened onto a conservatory containing a fountain. The interior was richly furnished and decorated in the lavish style of the time; the third floor housed the author's famous red billiard room, which opened onto a hexagonal fretted balcony that has been likened to a paddleboat's pilothouse. Tuckerman was influenced by the writings of Ruskin, but the flamboyance of the design probably owed something to Clemens himself, who actively participated in its making and who, with characteristic grandiloquence, often referred to himself as its architect.

This gaudy commemoration of Victorian domesticity—and of Clemens's celebrity—was "part steamboat, part medieval household, and part cuckoo clock," wrote one biographer. Many people would have been overwhelmed by these surroundings, but Clemens (who coined the term "Gilded Age") loved luxury, and the opulence suited him—and his alter ego, Mark Twain—perfectly. He moved there with his family in 1875, and it was his home for the next two decades.

In the nineteenth century it was not unusual for a successful writer to build a house for himself, although few lavished as much money on their homes as Clemens, whose architectural extravagance drove him to bankruptcy. In this he was anticipated by an earlier celebrated writer-builder, Sir Walter Scott. In 1811, Scott acquired a hundred-acre farm alongside the Tweed, in the Scottish Border country, with the intention of building a house. He named the property Abbotsford, to commemorate the ancient abbots of

Melrose, who had once owned these lands, and the nearby place where an old Roman road had once forded the river.

Scott started with modest plans and engaged a Glasgow architect to prepare a design for an unassuming cottage, similar in size to the rented farmhouse that he had been living in at Ashestiel. The writer's enthusiasm for building surfaced immediately, and he elaborated his requirements until the projected "cottage" resembled a large country house. The contractor's estimates proved too expensive, and the plans—together with their architect—were set aside. Instead, Scott and his family moved into an old stone house that was already on the property. They were crowded in the small dwelling, but with Scott's fortune on the rise, he was able, six years later, to think of enlarging his home.

This time he decided to build, not, as before, a brand-new house, but a wing that linked the farmhouse to a nearby structure known as the Chapel, which contained several guest rooms. This sounds modest, but the extension, which was designed by a London architect, William Atkinson, grew to include a large dining room, a study, a conservatory, and an armory for Scott's sizable collection of guns and military curios. That was on the lower level; the upper floor contained two large bedrooms and a dressing room. The combination of old and new construction produced a rambling effect, very different from the earlier design. This appealed to Scott: "I have always had a private dislike to a regular shape of house although no doubt it would be wrong headed to set about building an irregular one from the beginning," he wrote to his young friend Daniel Terry, an actor who had trained as an architect and to whom Scott regularly turned for architectural advice.

In 1822, Scott began a second and more ambitious expansion to his home. Since his move to Abbotsford, his literary fame had grown even more bright, he had been knighted, and publishers were paying him unprecedented sums for anything he would write. His building plans expanded accordingly. The new wing was twice as large as its predecessor and required completely razing the old farmhouse. Abbotsford now included, in addition to several more bedrooms, a drawing room and spacious entrance hall, a large library (about the size of my original boatbuilding workshop), a study, and, attached to it, an octagonal oratory. But it was its appearance as much as its size that impressed visitors. Atkinson's original design had been in the fashionable neo-Gothic style, which Scott thought artificial, and with the help of his young architect friend Edward Blore, he reworked the façades, "Scottifying" them, as he put it.*

Even before Scott started building, his friends began calling him "the Laird of Abbotsford." This was said in jest; but the celebrated writer, who was now his country's national bard, adopted this role with great seriousness and devoted his considerable energies to realizing an appropriately lairdly home. What had started as a cottage, and had grown into a country house, was now transformed into a fortresslike manor, with turrets, towers, and castellated gables—the first example of what was to become known as the Scottish Baronial Style, which was later given royal endorsement by Queen Victoria at Balmoral.

The Irish novelist Maria Edgeworth visited Abbotsford

---

* Blore, Scott's protégé, later achieved prominence as a champion of the Tudor Gothic style. He was also the architect of the east front of Buckingham Palace.

in 1823 and observed cheekily about the house: "All the work is so solid you would never guess it was by a castle-building romance writer & poet." In fact, romance and castle building were much in evidence. The house was a historical pastiche, composed of new pieces and old. The outside porch was based on that of the castle of Linlithgow; the chimneypiece in the hall was copied from the Abbot's Stall at Melrose Abbey. There were a large number of architectural fragments taken from old buildings and incorporated into the structure. In the garden stood a fountain that had been moved from Edinburgh; the wainscoting of the hall was from a ruined abbey. The walls, inside and out, were decorated with heraldic devices, coats of arms, and armorial shields.

Does it all sound a bit like Hearst's castle in San Simeon? Scott's father was a lawyer, not an aristocrat (his grandfather had been a prosperous sheep farmer); and the social pretensions of Abbotsford do recall Casa Grande. The escutcheons on the walls of the entrance hall belonged to Scott's family but included those of other clans and even of his friends. Like Hearst, Scott entertained on a grand scale. And like the newspaper magnate, he was a voracious collector. He owned twenty thousand books, many of them rarities. The house, which must have resembled a museum, was crammed with curious fragments of history—battle relics of Culloden and Waterloo, Rob Roy's gun, Napoleon's pistols, a clock that had belonged to Marie Antoinette, a writing desk made out of wood from a wrecked galleon of the Spanish Armada. Like Casa Grande, Abbotsford was an expression of individualism and a monument to its owner's will. "Scott's character was not a mere appearance," writes Edgar Johnson in his monumental biography, "it was a reality, because it was the man he wanted and was determined to be. It was a heroic structure sustained against all pressures by heroic resolution."

More than one house is associated with another Scottish novelist, Robert Louis Stevenson: the Edinburgh terrace house on Heriot Row in which he spent his childhood; Siron's Inn, an "artists' barrack" in Barbizon; the Grez pension where he met Fanny; the deserted miner's hut in the Napa Valley where they spent their honeymoon, and which was the setting for "The Silverado Squatters"; the Braemar cottage where he started *Treasure Island;* Skerryvore, in Bournemouth, his longest stopover (three years), where he wrote *Kidnapped.* Stevenson had a hereditary lung weakness, and he spent most of his short life avoiding the dampness and chill of his native and beloved Scotland. The search for a curative climate took him from one place to another. His ailment was never precisely diagnosed, and he tried all sorts of environments; he even spent a windy winter in a cabin at Saranac Lake. In his ten years of marriage he changed abodes more than fifteen times, sometimes staying only a few months before his recurring illness—and a restlessness of spirit—drove him on. "It was as though Fate was not going to let Louis settle permanently anywhere until he reached his journey's end in the South Seas," wrote James Pope Hennessy.

In 1890 the Stevensons, traveling on a rented schooner in Polynesia, arrived in Western Samoa, and, finding the climate congenial, they decided it was time to stop wandering. They looked for a house, but these were on the coast, where they felt it would be unhealthy. Instead they bought a three-hundred-acre parcel of land high in the mountains, intending to make it into a plantation and their home. "The place is beautiful beyond dreams," Stevenson wrote to a close friend, "some fifty miles of the Pacific spread in front; deep woods all around; a mountain making in the sky a profile of huge trees upon our left." He called it Vailima, "the place of five streams."

Stevenson was a romantic and an idealistic dreamer, but this attitude did not extend to houses. In an letter to Henry James, extolling his life cruising the South Seas, he had written, "I was never fond of . . . houses." Nevertheless, at Vailima he immersed himself in the construction of his home to a greater extent than the wealthier Scott and Clemens. "I have been all day correcting proofs, and making out a new plan for our house," he wrote in a Christmas Eve letter to a friend. "The other was too dear to be built now, and it was a hard task to make a smaller house that would suffice for the present, and not be a mere waste of money in the future." Three days later he described "disputing, and consulting about brick and stone and native and hydraulic lime, and cement and sand, and all sorts of otiose details about the chimney—just what I fled from in my father's offices twenty years ago; I should have made a languid engineer."

His earlier training in engineering is evidenced in Vailima, which had none of the fantasy of Abbotsford, and none of the whimsy of the Hartford house. In its final form (royalties permitted Stevenson finally to enlarge it) the house consisted of two large, rectangular, undecorated blocks, and it has often been likened to a barn. It must have given that impression, at least from the exterior, with its corrugated-iron roof painted red and its peacock-blue siding. The straightforward shape recalled Stevenson's grandfather's house, Colinton Manse, a place of many happy childhood memories.

Vailima had no architectural pretensions, but it was

suited to the Polynesian climate. The wooden structure was enclosed on both floors by deep verandas, from which one could see the port of Apia below. The tall rooms had plenty of windows, which were eventually equipped with a recent innovation: flyscreens. The building fitted in, but it was by no means primitive—it was not built in the native style. All the materials—iron roofing, wood, nails, and window glass—were imported from either Australia or the United States. The ground floor of one block contained a spacious hall, whose walls and ceiling were paneled in California redwood and which was fitted with large glazed sliding doors. A broad staircase led to the second floor, which was divided into bedrooms. The furniture—including a piano —as well as the pictures, silverware, and glassware, had been shipped from Scotland; so had the contents of his library. The cast-iron cookstove came from America. In the dining room Stevenson had allowed himself a reminder of his homeland: a brick fireplace, the only one on the island.

Stevenson lived in his house until his death—only four years—but judging from his letters he became greatly attached to "my beautiful, shining, windy house." There is a famous photograph of Vailima taken in 1892. Fifteen persons are grouped on the front steps of the veranda. The writer is flanked by the two important women of his life: Fanny and his widowed mother, who had arrived at Vailima the year before. The three sit on chairs; the rest stand or lounge on the steps. Fanny's grown-up son, Lloyd, and her daughter, Belle, are there, as is Belle's ne'er-do-well husband, Joe Strong, and their young son. Except for Belle's English maid, the others are Samoan members of the Stevenson household: Lafaele, the house steward; Talolo, the cook; the two table boys. It is a curious group: a stern Fanny in a heavy brocaded dress; an elderly lady who resembles Queen Victoria; Lloyd in laced-up boots and slouch hat like a nineteenth-century explorer; the prim maid; and the dark Samoans in lavalavas and flowered leis. Joe Strong stands moodily apart (he would shortly abandon Belle), but there is an intimacy among the rest of the people that turns what might have been an exotic scene into a familial, domestic one. The photographer has placed Stevenson at the center of the scene, which is proper. As in all his painted portraits and photographs, he is unsmiling; but if the Calvinist bohemian does not radiate happiness, he does look content.

Stevenson admired Scott, and in one of his letters he jokingly called his tropical estate "Subpriorsford"; his young Samoan employees became known as the "Vailima men," and on Sundays Stevenson had them wear Royal Stuart lavalavas, but that too was his wry humor. Vailima, unlike Abbotsford, was not a memorial to its owner. The wandering writer had been at home in many different places, and, as his house so well demonstrated, he was a master at fitting in. At Vailima, he became involved in local politics, socialized with Samoan royalty, gave traditional feasts, and wrote a history of the islands. Little wonder that when he died, forty chiefs cut a road to the top of Mount Vaea and carried his coffin to his chosen resting place.

Stevenson's finances had constrained him to a parcel of land that, although large, was physically daunting; Vailima had a melodious name and a beautiful view, but otherwise it was impassable jungle. Much effort was required to domesticate this tropical landscape, work into which Stevenson threw himself with enthusiasm. "I am a mere farmer," he wrote to the editor of *Scribner's*. "My talk, which would scarce interest you on Broadway, is all of fuafua and tuitui, and black boys, and planting and weeding, and axes and cutlasses; my hands are covered with blisters and full of thorns; letters are, doubtless, a fine thing, so are beer and skittles, but give me farmering in the tropics for real interest." "*Nothing* is so interesting as weeding," he wrote to Sidney Colvin, in London. He was obviously pulling his friend's leg, but the jest masked an enduring truth. Transforming a site, whether it is a piece of Samoan jungle or a Canadian meadow, means leaving lasting marks of habitation in a previously unoccupied place—it is the greatest satisfaction of housebuilding.

ຯ   ຯ   ຯ

George Bernard Shaw was largely indifferent to his physical surroundings—his house at Ayot Saint Lawrence, where he lived during the last forty-four years of his long life, was a nondescript Victorian rectory. But Shaw too was a builder, and the writing room that he erected in his garden was a Shavian combination of simplicity, convenience, and novelty. He called it "the Shelter," but it was really a shed, only eight feet square. It contained the essentials of the writer's trade—a plank desk, an electric lamp, a wicker chair, a bookcase, and a wastepaper basket. Beside the desk was a shelf for his Remington portable—like Clemens, Shaw was an early amateur of the typewriter. There was also a telephone (modified to refuse incoming calls), a thermometer, and an alarm clock (to remind him when it was time for lunch). Inside the door was a mat where the fastidious writer wiped his shoes. The shed was austere—a vegetarian's workplace, one might say; the pine boards and framing were painted white on the inside and left to weather on the exterior. The door, which was placed in the center of the wall, included a glass pane and had a fixed window on each side; a small window on the rear wall opened for ventilation.

The Shelter incorporated an unusual technical feature. Shaw wrote in the morning, and it was to warm the unheated interior that he had located almost all the glazed openings on one side. To increase the effectiveness of these windows, he devised a curious solution: instead of resting on a foundation, the floor was supported on a central steel pipe, which permitted the entire room to be manually turned, like a revolving Victorian bookstand. This way, Shaw could benefit from the morning sun at different times of year. According to his secretary, however, the hut was never rotated; once it was loaded with furniture and books, it was probably too heavy to move.

Shaw's solitary shed recalls Samuel Clemens's tiny, freestanding octagonal study on a windy hilltop at Quarry Farm. It was there, and not in his luxurious but distracting house, that Clemens did most of his writing, including *The Adventures of Tom Sawyer* and *Huckleberry Finn*. The elegant little gazebo, which had windows on all sides and a contrived fireplace with two chimneys and a window over the mantelpiece, was built for Clemens by his sister-in-law and was almost certainly professionally designed. On the other hand, Shaw's shed, his secretary assured, was "entirely his own idea."

Another house that was entirely of its owners' making was the home of the Swedish artists Carl and Karin Larsson. The building of the Larssons' house took place over a long period of time, and in an extemporaneous fashion that recalled my own construction odyssey. In 1889, they had received as a gift from Karin's father a small log cabin in the village of Sundborn in central Sweden. This traditional three-room, sixteen-foot-wide longhouse stood on a forlorn slag heap beside the Sundborn River. "But I called it my own," wrote Larsson, and it was an excuse to return to Sweden from France, where the two painters had been living for several years. At first, the cottage was used exclusively as a summer retreat and underwent only minor modifications. After a year, however, a small studio was built against one side. The house remained this way for the next ten years, until Larsson, more prosperous now, and with larger commissions, needed a more spacious room for painting. He built a large studio—at that time the largest in Sweden—at right angles to the house but detached from it (for privacy) and with proper, north-facing windows. The old studio was turned into a family room.

The following year, the Larssons decided to make the summer house their permanent home. Since their household now included seven children and two domestics, they added an extension that connected the house and the studio and included three additional bedrooms and a bathroom. The construction was carried out by a local carpenter and bricklayer, supervised largely by Karin Larsson, whose husband was often called away to paint in Stockholm and elsewhere. Nine years later, with the children older, the upper part of the studio was converted into individual bedrooms. The last addition, in 1912, was an old cottage that was moved from a neighboring village and attached to the end wall of the studio.

These varied expansions and additions produced a rambling house that incorporated a haphazard and carefree mixture of materials: logs, whitewashed stucco, painted wood siding, clay tiles, and tin roofing. Windows were placed more according to interior convenience than according to exterior composition; chimneys popped out as required. The result was architecturally unpretentious. The Larssons called their home Lilla Hyttnäs—the Hut on a Point—and it was definitely a series of sheds, not a cathedral.

We know a great deal about life at Lilla Hyttnäs as a result of a series of detailed watercolors that Carl Larsson began painting around 1900. They depicted charming scenes of everyday family life: household chores, a birthday party, the girls dressing for Sunday church, Carl and Karin in the darkened sitting room after the children have gone to bed. The first of this series portrayed his son Pontus sitting unhappily in the "punishment corner." But what a corner! Beside Pontus stood an eighteenth-century tile oven, whose floral ornament had spilled over onto the adjacent wall. The walls were peach-colored, the moldings were green; the scrubbed floor of unadorned planks was plain wood. As in a rococo interior, the over-door panel and the door itself had been decorated by Larsson with paintings. The upper panel of the door contained a tongue-in-cheek poem, curiously in English: "There was a little woman who lived with C.L.,/And if she is not gone she lives there still— very well." Karin—the "little woman"—was depicted in the lower panel.

Throughout the house the rooms were brightly decorated with a painter's palette: orange doors and yellow window frames, green ceilings and ocher-yellow walls. The furniture was an eclectic mixture of old and new: rococo chairs painted white or blue; a canopied bed built by Carl Larsson; a baroque cupboard nonchalantly decorated with a painting of one of his daughters; children's beds designed by Karin.

Antique paneling was comfortably placed beside simple handweaving. Aphorisms and sayings (some humorous, some serious) adorned the walls.

In 1899, Carl Larsson published the first of several illustrated books about his house: *Ett Hem* (At Home). Two other books followed, but it was a German anthology, *Das Haus in der Sonne* (The House in the Sun), that attracted an international public. His delicately drafted depictions of family life, and especially the delightful architectural settings that praised domesticity in an unassuming but picturesque manner, captivated his readers. Lilla Hyttnäs became famous; according to art historian Peter Thornton, "No other house in the world can have been so widely publicized, and the influence of these pictures was enormous."

The cheerful colors, the bright and sun-filled interiors, and the simple forms of the Larssons' home prefigured a more natural approach to interior decoration. There is no doubt that the Larssons were interested in making an aesthetic point—hence the illustrated books. But although artistry was involved, they never permitted themselves to treat their house as a work of art; it was a *home*. There was nothing precious about Lilla Hyttnäs, which the descendants of the Larssons still use as a summer house.

This house is my favorite. It achieved the domesticity of Clemens's home and the personality of Abbotsford with considerably less effort and fanfare. It grew, piece by piece, over an extended period of time and was modified and adapted to changing circumstances and to the changing lives of its occupants. If buildings are clothes, this house was like a worn and carefully patched jacket that has taken the shape of its wearer over time and become a sort of second skin. The Larssons inhabited—the word is apt—their home for thirty years. As it stands today, it demonstrates the third sense of "habit"—something customary and familiar, repeated daily, brought to fruition. It is evidence of how individuals can transform a place, and hence make it particular, not by grand design but by the small celebrations of everyday life.

A house such as Lilla Hyttnäs embodies the personality of its occupants; a more uncompromising design such as the Villa Rotonda discloses the preoccupations of its designer but reveals little about its owner. This is not to say that Palladio did not adapt his designs to the special needs of his patrons; but his designs—like those of Mies van der Rohe—were not improvised in response to the particularities of an individual client. For example, at about the same time as he was building the house for Almerico, Palladio was asked to design another hilltop residence, and he adopted a similar cruciform arrangement, with four porticoes and a central domed room. That his clients, the two Trissino brothers, were country gentry and not retired men of the cloth mattered little; the rules of Palladio's building game had been developed and refined over decades. That is also why Wright had been able to design the Fallingwater house so quickly—it was obviously something that he had been thinking about for some time previous.*

&ta. &ta. &ta.

An Italian architectural magazine recently sponsored an international competition that had a single requirement: to

---

* Wright also (openly) reused designs from earlier, unrealized commissions. When a house that he had planned for the Jacobs family in 1943 proved too expensive, he offered it to a Wisconsin neighbor, M. N. Hein. Hein died, and the house remained unbuilt, but the design was resurrected a third time as the Bloomfield house, this time in Arizona.

design "the most beautiful house in the world." What did I think that meant? a colleague asked me. That's easy, I said. The most beautiful house in the world is the one that you build for yourself.

Beauty was not the first thing that came to Ramón Castrejón's mind when he thought of his house. He was not a famous painter or a famous writer—not a famous anything, although he was a decent enough watchmaker to support his wife and four young children. He had his own stall in downtown Zihuatanejo, a town on the Pacific coast of Mexico, but even in that prosperous tourist region it had taken him some time to set aside enough savings to move his family out of their rented room. Like Scott and Stevenson, he was forty years old when he felt able to think of acquiring his own home; and, as with most prospective homeowners—even famous writers—the thing that was uppermost on his mind was money.

In 1985 he bought a parcel of land at Los Amusgos, a housing development not far from the center of town. "Housing development" is an inaccurate description of a bare piece of sloping land that had been subdivided into small rectangular plots; to most North Americans, the bleak layout at Los Amusgos would have looked like an unpleasant campground. There were half a dozen streetlamps and three public water taps, to be shared by two hundred and fifty families; there were no other services—no sewers or electricity—no trees, no landscaping, no sidewalks, no paving at all. But Castrejón, who had never seen a campground, considered himself lucky—he had a place to build.

The down payment for the land had exhausted Castrejón's savings, and it was only thanks to a loan from his wife's sister that he could begin to buy building materials.

In one corner of the plot he erected nine concrete columns; a one-inch layer of concrete on the ground served as a floor. On wood beams that spanned the columns he nailed corrugated, asphalted cardboard sheets; these would last five or six years, until he could afford to replace them with something more durable. The temporary walls were scavenged plastic sheeting, stretched between the columns. Four months after buying the land, just before New Year's Day, the family moved into their one-room dwelling.

Like the Larssons' home, their house grew piece by piece. As soon as possible, the plastic was replaced by light walls, made out of wooden slats that had originally been packing cases. There was a door but no windows. Then a long veranda roof, supported on wooden posts, was added against one wall, between the house and the street. The veranda and the wall inside it were painted a bright aquamarine. The next addition was a smaller room that served as a kitchen. By now more than half of the small plot was built upon. In a few years the Castrejóns, like their neighbors, acquired electricity (for the moment, illegally) and were able to buy a refrigerator, an electric fan, and a television set.

"If you hurry . . . a house, you are nearly sure to find out, by and by, that you have left out . . . a broom-closet, or some other little convenience," wrote Clemens; and he and Potter had spent a long time making sure that the Hartford house incorporated every amenity, including five (then novel) bathrooms. Even so, seven years after the house was complete, Clemens had the kitchen extended and all the interiors redecorated. The Castrejóns likewise continued to improve and expand. Three years after moving to Los Amusgos, they began to build two more rooms, but this

187

time out of brick and reinforced concrete. At the moment they have run out of money, and only part of the walls is finished. Bricks are being stockpiled for future construction; asbestos roofing sheets are temporarily used to enlarge the kitchen. Once the roof and a floor are complete, they plan to move most of their possessions there, and use the older rooms as a kitchen and room for the children.

Like Clemens, the Mexican family had decorated their home. The American writer could afford Louis Comfort Tiffany and Candace Wheeler; the posters and calendars that adorn the wood walls of the Castrejóns' single room are more modest, but the impulse is the same. There are pictures of the children in communion dress and of movie stars, and a magazine cover depicting Vicente Guerrero, a hero of the war of independence. A Christmas *piñata* hangs from the ceiling. The sofa and easy chairs are covered in improbable Scottish plaids. Although there are no coats of arms or escutcheons here, on one of the concrete posts, beneath the roughly marked house number, is a carefully painted figure of a little cat.

The house—most people would call it a shack—is not without artistry. Its long porch faces west; and to control the relentless sun, the side facing the street has been completely filled with creepers, ferns, flowers, and many types of herbs—*yerba buena* (for making tea), *hepazote,* and cilantro. Considering that water must be carried some distance from the public tap, the carefully tended plants are an accomplishment of some measure. Some are in plastic buckets and tin cans that stand on a low stone wall; others hang in containers from the roof beam. This lovely green curtain not only shades the hammocks and chairs within, it also gives privacy from the immediately adjacent street.

A concrete washbasin sits at one end of the wall—the youngest children use it as a play pool. Is it fanciful to call this house beautiful? It lacks the carefully orchestrated calm of the Villa Rotonda, or the breathtaking originality of Fallingwater, or the perfection of the Farnsworth house. Nevertheless, it exhibits something equally precious: the moving loveliness of human occupation, of a place transformed.

Like Shirley and me, Ramón Castrejón built his house himself, on weekends, and afternoons after work. He did this without professional help or advice, relying instead on a local building language, and on what John Habraken has called a "collective image" of the house. This collective image is culturally determined—in some places it is a longhouse, in others a cottage, in others a room with a veranda. It is an image that often eludes architects, who are more interested in innovation than in repetition. It is nevertheless something that is carried within us. The expression and recreation of this image was once a commonplace event, so ordinary it escaped the attention of the historians—hence the lack of interest in "sheds." Building your own home—and inhabiting a space of your own making—is considered by most to be a luxury.* It may yet be rediscovered to be more essential than that.

        ᴥ   ᴥ   ᴥ

"If I were asked to name the chief benefit of the house," wrote Gaston Bachelard, "I should say: the house shelters daydreaming." When I first read this, I thought that it was

---

* Paradoxically, it is a luxury that almost all poor people in the so-called underdeveloped world enjoy.

one of those obscure conceits that characterize certain kinds of self-consciously intellectual books. On reflection, however, it is a perfectly sensible notion. For where else, if not in the home, can we let our imagination wander? Not at work—neither in the office nor in the factory—nor in a busy street. Maybe, briefly, in a park, before we are accosted by a panhandler or, worse, a pamphleteer. Students daydream in class at their peril. It is dangerous, too, to fall into a reverie when driving a car (although I do it regularly), and planes are too noisy and cramped; trains are more conducive to musing—at least they used to be before neglect and organizational apathy set in. Except for churches, there are few places in the modern metropolis suitable for contemplation; that may be why we periodically go to the seaside. But few of us can live on the beach, so home it is. We say that we are happy to be home, and is that not what we mean—that we are in a familiar and comforting place, a place where it is safe to let our minds drift?

It was no coincidence that Stevenson, Scott, Clemens, Larsson, Castrejón, and I were less than forty years old when we built our homes. This was only partly a question of finances. The process of building, for all of us, was a process of installing ourselves in a place, of establishing a spot where it would be safe to dream. We had to be old enough to recognize the particularity—and limits—of our dreams, but not too old to believe in them.

The house contains our dreams, but it is also contained by them—which is to say that our houses take life in our imaginations, or, as an analyst might say, in our unconscious. That is why the places that people have fashioned for themselves are more touching than those—no matter how splendid—that others have made for them. Stevenson's unassuming generosity and Larsson's quirky humor are evidenced in the fabric of the homes they constructed. If I examine my own house I can see not only the reflection of someone who wants to fit in, but a guarded and diffident exterior—a little barn—that conceals a rich and complicated inner structure of small rooms that are neither totally enclosed nor totally open; an interior that is almost devious in its undramatic complexity.

A striking description of a house as an extension of the unconscious has been provided by the great psychologist Carl Jung. Jung had built a country retreat at Bollingen, on the shores of the upper lake of Zurich. During the protracted building process, which in all lasted thirty-two years, he several times enlarged and modified the house. There was no master plan; and if the completed house resembled a fairy-tale castle, this was more accidental than intentional, although Jung's taste in architecture was traditional.* Bollingen was intended to be archaic—there was no telephone, electricity, or running water; it was a place to return to a simpler life. The Swiss psychologist surrounded himself with symbols of the past. Into the stone walls of the courtyard he set several stone tablets, carved by himself: one was inscribed with the names of his antecedents and their family crest, another with an alchemical saying in Latin, a third with a mandala of Jung's own design.

Looking back, Jung described the completed house as "a kind of representation in stone of my innermost thoughts."

---

* An English visitor to Jung's permanent home in nearby Kussnacht once asked him: "Is this an old house?" "No," he answered, "but built after an ancient style." In fact the house had been built by Jung himself, at the age of thirty, and remained his home for more than fifty years.

He had begun, in 1923, with a low, circular dwelling that was intended to resemble an African hut and which he called "the maternal hearth." This eventually became a two-story structure, and four years later it was joined by a second, square tower. In time, a "spiritual tower" with a secluded meditation room was added, and lastly a walled courtyard linked the three parts. Judging from photographs, it was a clumsy composition, and so it remained for two decades, until the death of his wife. Jung had originally started the house shortly after his mother's demise; and once again, to still his grief, he began to build. "I suddenly realized that the small central section which crouched so low, so hidden, was myself! I could no longer hide myself behind the 'maternal' and the 'spiritual' towers." The result was a tall, striking, half-timbered upper story that dominated the two towers and successfully completed the composition. Jung was quick to admit that he was not immediately aware of this symbolism. "During the building work, of course, I never considered these matters. I built the house in sections, always following the concrete needs of the moment. It might also be said that I built it in a kind of dream."

Mr. Jung had built his dream house, not to realize a lifelong wish—not to make a "perfect" home—but as the unintentional expression of his private imaginings. I too had built a house piece by piece, according to what I thought were practical demands. But was I not, likewise, responding to a less evident agenda? As a child, I had lived in six houses, in three countries, on two continents. Since then I had occupied seven different homes. I had dreamt of a boat, and escape; but had I not always been running away, or at least moving away? Each shovel of gravel, each nail hammered, each board sawn, settled me more firmly in the meadow with the Azure Dragon on the left and the White Tiger on the right. My house had begun with the dream of a boat. The dream had run aground—I was now rooted in place.

ACKNOWLEDGMENTS

This book has had a long gestation. My first sketches of a boatbuilding shed are dated September 1975—they show a narrow building next to a tree. That was why when I saw the meadow and the old apple tree, I knew it was the right place to build. It was another five years before we moved

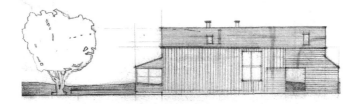

THE BOATHOUSE, 1982

to the finished house. In May 1986, in a room in Guesthouse Number Two of Tianjin University, I told the story of my house to a fellow visitor, a Belgian engineer. "You must write about this," he said; my thanks to Etienne Jamoulle for planting the seed. I thought that this would be an easy book to write, or at least a straightforward one. Instead it has taken many unexpected twists and turns, into archi-

ACKNOWLEDGMENTS

tectural, historical, and private pasts whose boundaries have sometimes become blurred. Like the building that it describes, this personal reflection has followed no grand design, and also like it, it has depended on the assistance of others. Specially, and throughout, Shirley Hallam; Dan Frank, my editor at Viking and perceptive critic; Carl Brandt, agent, counselor, and friend; and the helpful staffs of McGill University's Blackader-Lauterman Library of Art and Architecture and of the McLennan Graduate Library. This is also a convenient place to thank those friends who left the imprint of their labors, large and small, in the fabric of my building enterprise: Vikram Bhatt, Jean-Louis Béviere, Bernard and Danielle Lefebvre, Louise Bérubé, Donald Chen, Tom Clelland, and Mike Distaulo.

July 1988
The Boathouse
Hemmingford, Quebec

NOTES ON SOURCES

This reflective work is not intended to be a scholarly study, and I have refrained from providing detailed bibliographic references. Nevertheless, since I have relied on many books and articles, and for readers who wish to pursue a subject further, I am including some brief notes.

1: WIND AND WATER

Nikolaus Pevsner's *An Outline of European Architecture* (Penguin, 1943) is deservedly well known and still available in paperback. The Ruskin quotation is from his *Collected Works* (John W. Lovell, 1885). Daniel J. Boorstin's essay appeared in *Hidden History: Exploring Our Secret Past* (Harper & Row, 1987). The references to Gothic architecture are from Bernard Berenson's *Aesthetics and History* (Constable, 1950), B. G. Morgan's *Canonic Design in English Medieval Architecture* (Liverpool University Press, 1961), Erwin Panofsky's classic *Gothic Architecture and Scholasticism* (Meridian Books, 1957), Cecil Stewart's *Gothic Architecture* (Longmans, 1961), and Eric Mercer's *English Vernacular Houses* (Her Majesty's Stationery Office, 1975). The main source of information on Chinese necromancy was Ernest John Eitel's *Feng Shui*, published in 1873 and recently reprinted by Pentacle Books (Bristol, 1979). The Baptist missionary D. C. Graham recounted the story of the unlucky-lucky farmer in *The Chinese Recorder* (Vol. 67, No. 3, 1936); an earlier issue of the same journal (Vol. 51, No. 12, 1920) contains the essay by Lucius Chapin Porter. The Reverend J. Edkins wrote in the *Chinese Recorder and Missionary Journal* (Vol. 4, No. 10, 1872). The use of *feng-shui* in contemporary Hong Kong is described in *Architectural Record* (September 1985), the *International Herald Tribune* (June 2, 1987), and *Time* (June 22, 1987).

2: THE BUILDING GAME

Pieter Brueghel's *Children's Games* is analyzed by Sandra Hindman in *The Art Bulletin* (Vol. 43, No. 3, 1981). For historical background on children I have relied on Philippe Ariès's masterly *Centuries of Childhood: A Social History of Family Life* (Knopf, 1962), and for Dutch games, on Mary Francis Durantini's *The Child in Seventeenth-Century Dutch Painting* (UMI Research Press, 1983) and Simon Schama's *The Embarrassment of Riches: An Interpretation of Dutch Culture in the Golden Age* (Knopf, 1987). Information on specific games is contained in Edouard Fournier's *Histoire des Jouets et des Jeux d'Enfants*, published in Paris in 1889, H. G. Wells's 1912 monograph *Floor Games* (Arno Press, 1976), Gwen White's *Antique Toys: and Their Backgrounds* (Arno Press, 1971), and David Owen's informative essay "Where Toys Come From," in *The Atlantic Monthly* (Vol. 258, No. 4, 1986). Anyone interested in Chardin will enjoy Philip Conisbee's beautifully illustrated book *Chardin* (Phaidon, 1986). Froebel's house-song is from his *Pedagogics of the Kindergarten* (Appleton, 1900);

other information is from his *Autobiography* (Swan Sonnenschein & Co., 1903). Johan H. Huizinga's *Homo Ludens: A Study of the Play-Element in Culture* (Beacon Press, 1955) is as pertinent today as when it was written. The Lutyens quote is from *Sir Edwin Lutyens: Country Houses* (Whitney Library of Design, 1981). Bettelheim's "The Importance of Play" appeared in *The Atlantic Monthly* (Vol. 259, No. 3, 1987). Jung's story of building play is contained in his *Memories, Dreams, Reflections* (Pantheon Books, 1973).

3: MAKING SPACE

Information on Frank Lloyd Wright, here and elsewhere, is from his own *An Autobiography* (Horizon, 1943) and *The Natural House* (New American Library, 1970), Edgar Tafel's *Apprentice to Genius: Years with Frank Lloyd Wright* (McGraw-Hill, 1979), and Brendan Gill's biography *Many Masks* (G. P. Putnam's Sons, 1987). Peter Collins's article on the Gastronomic Analogy first appeared in the *RAIC Journal* (No. 38, 1961) and was reprinted in his perspicacious study *Changing Ideals in Modern Architecture, 1750–1950* (McGill University Press, 1965). I used Morris Hicky Morgan's translation of Vitruvius's *Ten Books of Architecture* (Dover, 1960), James Leoni's translation of Alberti's *Ten Books on Architecture* (Alec Tiranti, 1965), and Isaac Ware's translation of Palladio's *The Four Books of Architecture* (Dover, 1965).

4: FITTING IN

The founding of Montreal is recounted by François Dollier de Casson, a Sulpician priest who wrote *A History of Montreal, 1640–1672* (J. M. Dent & Sons, 1928) in 1672–73. Paul Marchant describes the Nabdam ceremony in *Shelter II* (Random House, 1978), an interesting source of information for owner-builders. The history of city-founding rites is documented by Joseph Rykwert in *The Idea of a Town: The Anthropology of Urban Form in Rome, Italy and the Ancient World* (Princeton University Press, 1976). Analogous Hindu rites are described by Prasanna Kumar Acharya in *Indian Architecture According to the Manasara-Silpasastra*, published in Bombay (Oxford University Press, 1927).

5: JUST A BARN

Sir Casimir's barn is mentioned by Eric Arthur and Dudley Witney in *The Barn: A Vanishing Landmark* (A & M Visual Library, 1972); additional information was provided by Peter Gzowski. *The Barn* is an admirable illustrated history of a neglected building type; so is Eric Sloane's delightfully eccentric *An Age of Barns* (Funk & Wagnalls, 1967). I also relied on John Martin Robinson's *Georgian Model Farms: A Study of Decorative and Model Farm Buildings in the Age of Improvement, 1700–1846* (Clarendon Press, 1983), Thomas Hubka's exemplary *Big House, Little House, Back House, Barn: The Connected Farm Buildings of New England* (University Press of New England, 1984), Robert Lionel Séguin's *Les Granges du Québec du XVIIe au XIXe Siècle* (Les Editions Quinze, 1976), and Charles Higounet's *La Grange de Vaulerent: Structure et exploitation d'un terroir cistercien de la plaine de France XIIe–XVe siècle* (Ecole Pratique des Hautes Etudes, 1965). The description of a circular-ribbed riding-house is from C. J. Richardson's *The Englishman's House: From a Cottage to a Mansion* (John Camden Hotten, 1870). Information on other famous barns was gleaned from *Mount Vernon: Washington's*

NOTES ON SOURCES

Home and the Nation's Shrine (Doubleday, 1916), by Paul Wilstach; *Mr. Jefferson, Architect* (Viking, 1973), by Desmond Guiness and Julius Trousdale Sadler, Jr.; and *H. H. Richardson: Complete Architectural Works* (MIT Press, 1984), by Jeffrey Karl Ochsner. The drawings of Van Horne's barn are preserved in McGill University's Canadian Architecture Collection.

6: CHRYSALIS

The Wright sledgehammer quote is from *Building with Frank Lloyd Wright* (Chronicle Books, 1978), a fascinating memoir by a two-time client, Herbert Jacobs. The movable mock-up of the Kroller house is described by Franz Schulze in *Mies van der Rohe: A Critical Biography* (University of Chicago Press, 1985). Thomas Jefferson's so-called honeymoon cottage is documented in Lester Walker's charming book *Tiny Houses* (Overlook Press, 1987). Information on traditional longhouses is largely from Eric Mercer's *English Vernacular Houses* and from *A History of Private Life, Volume II: Revelations of the Medieval World* (Harvard University Press, 1988), edited by Georges Duby.

7: THE MIND'S EYE

The Julia Child quotation is from a detailed examination of this illustrious cook's kitchen by Bill Stumpf and Nicholas Polites in *Design Quarterly* (No. 104, 1977). Serlio's unpublished domestic treatise has recently been edited by Myra Nan Rosenfeld as *Sebastiano Serlio on Domestic Architecture* (Architectural History Foundation, 1978). Information on the

Centre Pompidou is contained in *Architectural Design* (Vol. 47, No. 2, 1977), which devoted an entire issue to this building. *Signs, Symbols, and Architecture* (John Wiley, 1980) contains several interesting essays on the sign language of buildings, particularly "Function and Sign" by Umberto Eco, whom I have quoted several times. I have also relied on George Hersey's fascinating study *The Lost Meaning of Classical Architecture: Speculations on Ornament from Vitruvius to Venturi* (MIT Press, 1988). Buildings as mnemonic devices are discussed by Jonathan D. Spence in *The Memory Palace of Matteo Ricci* (Viking, 1984). Donald A. Norman describes the relationship between human behavior and the design of doors, light switches, and other common devices in *The Psychology of Everyday Things* (Basic Books, 1988).

8: The Most Beautiful House in the World

Rudolf Wittkower's *Architectural Principles in the Age of Humanism* (Tiranti, 1952) and *Palladio* (Penguin, 1966) and *Palladio's Villas* (J. J. Augustin, 1967), both by the noted Palladian scholar James S. Ackerman, served as the chief source on the Italian architect. The description of his own house by Samuel Clemens is contained in *Mark Twain's Letters* (Harper, 1917). The "part steamboat" quotation is from Justin Kaplan's *Mr. Clemens and Mark Twain* (Simon & Schuster, 1966); the octagonal study at Quarry Farm is described by Albert Bigelow Paine in *Mark Twain: A Biography* (Harper, 1912); an architectural analysis of the Hartford house is contained in Robert A. N. Stern's *Pride of Place* (Houghton Mifflin, 1986). Information on Abbotsford is from Edgar Johnson's *Sir Walter Scott: The Great Unknown* (Macmillan, 1970). Vailima is described in *The Vailima Letters* (Methuen, 1895) and *The Letters*

NOTES ON SOURCES

of Robert Louis Stevenson (Scribners, 1899), both edited by Stevenson's friend Sidney Colvin; Mrs. M. I. Stevenson's *Letters from Samoa, 1891–1895* (Methuen, 1906); and *Robert Louis Stevenson* (Jonathan Cape, 1974), by James Pope Hennessy. George Bernard Shaw's writing hut is described by his secretary, Blanche Patch, in *Thirty Years with G.B.S.* (Gollancz, 1951) and illustrated in Walker's *Tiny Houses*. The atmosphere at Lilla Hyttnäs is wonderfully conveyed by Karl-Erik Granath's photographs in *Carl Larsson's Home* (Addison-Wesley, 1978). I was unable to locate English translations of Larsson's books, although *A Home* (Putnam, 1974) and *Our Home* (Methuen, 1976) are delightful adaptations intended for children's reading; *The Paintings of Carl Larsson* (Scribner's, 1976) includes many views of Lilla Hyttnäs. The quote by Peter Thornton is from his *Authentic Decor: The Domestic Interior, 1620–1920* (Viking, 1984). The Castrejón family study is part of a research thesis that is being carried out by Jesus Navarrete, my graduate student at McGill University. John Habraken's study is *Transformations of the Site* (Awater Press, 1983); the statement by Gaston Bachelard is from *The Poetics of Space* (Beacon Press, 1964). Jung's country retreat is described in *Memories, Dreams, Reflections*. The episode of Jung and the English visitor is recounted by Patricia Hutchins in "The World of James Joyce," from *C. G. Jung Speaking: Interviews and Encounters* (Princeton University Press, 1977). The colleague who asked me about "the most beautiful house in the world," and inadvertently provided me with a title for this book, was Joseph Rykwert.

INDEX

Abbotsford, 172–76, 177, 179, 184
Académie Royale d'Architecture, 9
Adam, Robert, 106, 107, 108
Alberti, Leon Battista, 10, 55, 56, 57, 60, 62, 139
  on drawing, 121
  as humanist, 156–57
  on necessity, 63, 65, 148
  writings of, 52–54, 63
Alexander, Christopher, 60–62, 139
architect, etymology of, 23
architectural design, see design, architectural
Architectural Graphic Standards (Ramsey and Sleeper), 62–63, 147
architectural treatises, 50–67
  ancient, 50–52
  classical, 64–67
  in Low Countries, 58
  modern, 58–60, 82
  Renaissance, 52–58

theoretical, 60–64
Victorian, 58
architecture:
  ancient Greek, 155–56
  classical, 64–67, 155–56, 165–66
  construction toys and, 36; see also games and toys
  design of, see design, architectural
  functional vs. aesthetic, 3–6, 49–50, 63
  Georgian, 106–107
  Hindu, 78–79, 91n, 131, 158–59
  in India, 91–92
  meanings of, see meaning and architecture
  as profession, 21–24
  representation of, see drawing, architectural; representation
  vernacular, 10–11, 127
architecture schools, 9
Ariès, Philippe, 27

INDEX

INDEX

INDEX

INDEX

INDEX